Merry Christmas
Marsha! Happy
reading —
Love you
Kris
12-01

Canoe Country &
Snowshoe Country

The Fesler-Lampert Minnesota Heritage Book Series

This series is published with the generous assistance of the John K. and Elsie Lampert Fesler Fund and David R. and Elizabeth P. Fesler. Its mission is to republish significant out-of-print books that contribute to our understanding and appreciation of Minnesota and the Upper Midwest.

Canoe Country &
Snowshoe Country

Florence Page Jaques
Illustrations by Francis Lee Jaques

Foreword by Justine Kerfoot

University of Minnesota Press

Minneapolis – London

Canoe Country was first published in hardcover by the University of Minnesota Press in 1938.
Snowshoe Country was first published in hardcover by the University of Minnesota Press in 1944.

Published by the University of Minnesota Press
111 Third Avenue South, Suite 290
Minneapolis, MN 55401-2520
http://www.upress.umn.edu

A Cataloging-in-Publication record for this book is available from the Library of Congress.

Printed in the United States of America on acid-free paper

The University of Minnesota is an equal-opportunity educator and employer.

11 10 09 08 07 06 05 04 03 02 01 00 99   10 9 8 7 6 5 4 3 2 1

Foreword

Justine Kerfoot

I first met Florence and Lee Jaques in the fall of 1943 when they checked into Gunflint Lodge for an extended stay. Lee had lived in Minnesota as a boy and young adult, and Florence was a Midwesterner who had transplanted herself to New York City. Her only previous experience in Minnesota had been a honeymoon canoe trip some years before, an adventure she described with great enthusiasm and insight in *Canoe Country.* Now the Jaqueses were returning to introduce Florence to winter in the northwoods, and one of our cabins would be their winter home. All their meals would be with our family in either the lodge or our home. To say that this was a change in lifestyle from their home in New York City would be an understatement.

During the Jaqueses' stay, I introduced Florence to the winter woods by dog team and snowshoe. Her enthusiasm for and interest in everything around her was quickly apparent: Florence was game to try it all. In many ways she learned by watching me do my daily chores, such as setting a trap line or training my dog team. Sometimes we combined a dog-training session with a picnic lunch down the lake. Whatever we did, our constant companions were my two small children, Bruce and Patty. My overriding memory of these excursions is that tripping with Florence was fun. I was accustomed to showing guests around the northwoods and could spot when someone truly appreciated the woods as Florence did.

Lee spent much of his time painting. On a couple of occasions I watched him. It was very meticulous work and he was thoroughly engrossed in it. Those who watched stood back and tried not to break the spell; no one would ever think of asking a question. In between the tropical birds we saw him paint, Lee found time to sketch things around him. I never dreamed that anyone would want to draw the old barrel stove in his cabin, but it is one of my favorite drawings in *Snowshoe Country*.

Our long winter evenings were spent as an enlarged family. The children provided the normal entertainment and distraction, and after dinner the adults sat around to talk or play games. One night Florence and I had a painting contest with Lee as the judge. Each of us was to paint an easy subject—trees. Unfortunately, this was also a subject that Lee was an acknowledged expert at depicting. His considered opinion was that we both should stick to writing.

Eventually the Jaqueses' time with us came to an end. Although they had come from a large city and enjoyed the lifestyle of a young couple without children, during their time with us Florence and Lee became part of our family in the wilderness with two rambunctious children. How well they adapted is reflected by the fact that we were all sorry to be parting.

Several months after Florence and Lee had returned to New York, the Wilderness Express arrived with the weekly mail delivery. Gunflint Lodge served as a local post office for the neighbors on the lake, and they gathered early on mail days to visit over a cup of coffee. Bruce and Patty ran around catching the sense of anticipation from the adults. Dogs barked. Everyone was busy talking while keeping one eye on the road until, suddenly, the truck was here. There was a hurried exchange of freight and mail. A few words were passed with the driver about what was going on in town or further down the trail. Then, just as quickly, the truck was off again.

Sorting everything that had arrived was the next step. The lodge's pile contained an unexpected package from Florence, but there was no time to look at it when everyone else was waiting for me to finish sorting. After a short time the stragglers went home to read their mail and open their parcels, and a quiet moment descended upon the lodge.

Over a cup of coffee Bill and I opened the mail. Florence's intriguing package was a surprise that I had eagerly awaited a free moment to open. What was it? It turned out to be a manuscript. Totally unbeknownst to us, Florence had been writing a book during her visit to Gunflint and we were all in it. This really threw us for a loop.

Bill and I quickly scanned the pages to find ourselves appearing through someone else's eyes. It was an unnerving experience. Is that what we really looked like? The events are accurate and we did say all those things, but who would have thought that Florence was going to write them down? Who would want to read about us?

Looking back from a vantage point of fifty-some years, I know that lots of people found Florence's story captivating. She shared her apprehension of this world but she also took the time to look around and really see what winter life was all about. Gradually she learned to love and appreciate the winter woods. Lee's sketches offered just the right counterpoint so the reader could visualize the scene. We got used to people asking us questions about the events in the book—and Bruce, of course, spent many embarrassing years living down his attempt to warm a puppy by throwing it into the fire.

As I reread *Canoe Country* today, it dawns on me that for a brief moment Florence and I were on parallel paths through the Boundary Waters. The year she and Lee took their honeymoon canoe trip was just about the same time I was taking my first canoe trip out of Gunflint. I am impressed by Florence's ability to observe the animals around her and turn them into characters in nature's daily drama. On my first canoe trip I was too overwhelmed by all the newness around me to even consider writing it down. After our separate canoe trips, the Jaqueses' lives and mine went in different directions. They were on their way back to New York and museum life. I built my life in the northwoods.

The Boundary Waters was the land where I chose to live my life, raise my children, and establish their values. During the winter the children rode on my back in a tikinagan (an Indian cradleboard). Sometimes they were secured to a sled pulled by dogs across snow-covered lakes. Eventually they learned to strap on snowshoes and follow me through the woods. I tried to teach them the rhythms of life. All around us the beaver, mink, fox, wolves, pine marten, otter, and a myriad of other animals were teaching their young the act of survival.

Canoe Country and *Snowshoe Country* are two treasures of Minnesota literature that reveal the Jaqueses' love of the awe-inspiring majesty of the Boundary Waters. As Florence later wrote, "This is not an escape from reality—in fact, it is an awakening to what is reality." It is evident from the warmth and charm of Florence's writing and Lee's drawings that these were two people who had fun exploring. The magic comes from the way Florence and Lee combined their talents. Lee shows the country in black and white while Florence's descriptions abound with color. *Canoe Country* and *Snowshoe Country* are in many ways timeless, because so much of what the Jaqueses saw is still in the Boundary Waters for visitors to discover.

Gunflint Lodge
March 1999

Canoe Country

by

FLORENCE PAGE JAQUES

illustrations by

FRANCIS LEE JAQUES

LIST OF ILLUSTRATIONS

Canoe Country

New York
February 20th

"I'll always turn to the North!" said Lee.

He had been talking about the jungle trails on Barro Colorado Island, in Panama. Till my mind was a whirl of howling monkeys and motmots swinging, scarlet passion flowers and peccaries and blazing blue butterflies.

"Why don't we go to the tropics on our next vacation?"

"I'd rather show you the North," Lee insisted. "Alaska, the Aleutian Islands, Hudson Bay —"

"But the Arctic is either cold or swampy. I know I'd revel in constant balminess, and the bursts of tropic color — whole trees of golden blossoms, and faint rose —"

"Listen. I grant you the tropics are beautiful. But the design is too intricate. Now, in the North you may have one line for the tundra, one for a maroon hill, and another for the snow mountains. Only three lines in the whole landscape. But *what* lines they are! I tell you, the Arctic has character, and composition."

"Yes, my lamb, I know you like the Arctic. But *I* can't revel in starkness. I do want to see solitary places, Lee. But I want to be able to lie down on my back and look at the sky —"

9

"You can't lie down, or even sit down, out of doors in Panama. If you stop one minute, the ticks and red bugs get you."

"Oh —" I was rather baffled. "Anyway, I like trees."

Lee shook his head. "I'll have to take you to the southern limit of the North! What about my state? What about northern Minnesota sometime?"

"That's not arctic."

"It's not so far from it. The muskeg comes down there, and we certainly have winter weather. . . . I wish we could see it this minute; snow means something *there*." Lee looked with intense scorn at the perfectly adequate snow storm outside our windows, whirling around corners and blurring the towers far up the street quite recklessly enough, it seemed to me.

"I wish we were there now," he repeated. "I'd like you to see the pines and tamaracks in three feet of snow. You ought to hear the snow screech under the sled runners, and trees crack in the silence, at twenty below zero."

"I'll go in summer," I said firmly.

"Or early spring, with the horned larks on the fence posts along the snowy roads. Or October. We could hunt prairie chickens then, through the fields."

I began to think of all the things Lee had told me of his Minnesota home. The great stretches of woods where he had hunted deer in his boyhood. The immense skies. Seven Oaks, the house of hand-hewn logs, built by some pioneer and discovered by Lee's mother and father when they came to that country; a house set, with its oaks around it, in a deep curve of the Mississippi. The Mississippi itself, only a small river in that northern land, where Lee used to watch logs floating down to the mills, and the stern-wheeled steamers traveling in summer. The old state road, where the four-horse teams hauled provisions to the lumber camps all through the winter. . . .

10

"I do want to see Minnesota before it loses every trace of pioneer life. But I'll go in summer," I reiterated.

"Of course, if we went in summer I could take you into the Arrowhead country," Lee admitted.

"Yes! What about that canoe country? After all your tales and promises, Othello! Have you ever taken me?"

"Well, why not go? This summer?"

We looked at each other questioningly. Then hopefully.

Perhaps we really shall.

Sunday, February 27th

It has been raining furiously all day long. I'm glad it has.

This afternoon we unearthed the canoe country maps. Lee has shown them to me before and I've always looked at them with sedate interest — never with the catches of breath they gave me today.

There's one huge map of the lake country in general, all the way from the international boundary to the Arctic and from Lake Superior to the Lake of the Woods, nearly to Winnipeg. Another is a detailed map of the Arrowhead itself, the Quetico reserve in Canada and the Superior National Forest in Minnesota, the borderland of both countries. Then smaller maps, some of which Lee helped to make.

I can hardly believe in that country. Hundreds and hundreds of lakes scattered through forest, like pieces of a mammoth jigsaw puzzle scattered over a table. Scraps of rivers lace the lakes together. There are no roads, no paths except short portages; one can travel only by water.

We hung over the maps till I could see curled waves and minute pine trees all over them. I found "This Man's Lake" and "That Man's Lake," with a forlorn little "No Man's Lake" tucked in between and an "Other Man's Lake" farther on. We traced out all Lee's former canoe trips, and he showered me with incredible numbers of old snapshots, to illustrate his explanations. They were most beautiful photographs.

12

"Lee, we *must* go," I cried.

He disappeared, and came back, to my amazement, with a stepladder. It seemed a peculiar answer to my exclamation. Were we to take off immediately, with the stepladder for airplane? But no. Mounting it, he began to excavate the top recesses of the studio closet.

"What *are* you after?"

". . . see what I've saved from my equipment," he muttered, and began to hand down the canvas bundles and packsacks which have always been mysteries to me.

I don't know how we progressed from studio to living room, but soon we had the latter ornamented with a small tent, an axe, a bevy of pails that fitted into each other with marvelous precision, tin plates, scores of small cloth bags ("you carry all the food in those; you can't pack the extra weight of boxes and cans"), fishing tackle, a coffee pot, a skillet, besides the maps and pictures scattered like leaves after a storm.

13

Of course it had to be the immaculate Bartons who called at this moment, with two German ornithologists in tow. It couldn't have been any of our intimate acquaintances.

To brush aside Mrs. Barton's magnificent pretense that there was nothing at all extraordinary about our living room *décor*, we had to explain, "We're going on a canoe trip this summer."

So we are committed now. What fun!

Duluth, Minnesota
August 21st

I've never been so cold in my life. I wear my fur coat all the time. If this is what Duluth is like in August what must it be in January!

"Of course," people tell me cheerily, "you'll be much colder camping out."

And I can't take this fur coat with me.

"Three weeks!" they say. "And you've never camped before? Better make it one!"

Three weeks does take careful planning. We must remember everything; there is no place to buy or borrow. And to pack house and furnishings and food inside one small canoe is quite puzzling. Today we've been sorting out our equipment in Aunt Mary's garden, while the next-door children ran around and over us like beetles in wild excitement.

Lee's canoe is intact and is ready to ship to Winton. Our tent is so small it's laughable. Seven by seven, with a ground cloth to match, it ties up in front by one rope to a pole or tree. We're taking an air mattress, an air pillow, and a blanket roll.

There are three packsacks, one for food, another for clothes (with a waterproof bag that holds our toilet articles and a small medicine case), and a third for miscellaneous articles—fishing tackle, films, Lee's sketching outfit, my notebooks, canoe glue, an axe, flashlights, etc. We aren't allowed to take a gun.

We have gone over our list of provisions again and again. The **food** must be nourishing and yet as concentrated in bulk as it can possibly be. Each purchase is now neatly tied into its little cloth bag. Except the butter—it goes in a can. This is our list:

5 lbs ham	2 lbs salt (we salt the fish to keep it)
5 lbs bacon	
2 lbs dried beef	1 can pepper
1 can corned beef	4 lbs sweet chocolate
1 can veal loaf	2 lbs cheese
3 cans Crisco	2 cans soluble coffee
2 lbs butter	1 can lemon powder (for lemonade)
10 lbs flour	
1 can baking powder	5 lbs brown sugar (for syrup as well as sugar)
4 loaves bread	
1 package rye crisp	1 can powdered milk
2 lbs raisins	2 bars soap
3 lbs apricots	1 cake Sapolio
3 lbs prunes	6 candles
4 lbs dried beans	1 box matches (another in miscellaneous pack)
2 lbs dried peas (a mistake)	

It seems what the women's magazines might call a Meager Menu. Of course if we were taking a guide we could live much more luxuriously, with canned vegetables and even an oven. But a guide would bring civilization into our trip; we would have a buffer between us and the wilderness. As it is, we're facing nature as I, at least, never have before in my life.

As for reading, I'm afraid I'm going to do less of that in the next few weeks than I've ever done in the same length of time. I have three paper-bound reprints, and an old copy of *The King's Henchman*, which hasn't any cover!

I did want to take along some of the vivid stories of explorers and fur

traders, especially the earliest ones, Radisson and Du Luth, for instance, and La Vérendrye (Pierre Gaultier de Varennes de la Vérendrye, to be exact), who with his sons built a string of forts along this route.

Most of all I wanted to take the account Radisson wrote for some of his patrons in England. Radisson was a dashing scamp, perhaps the first white man ever to set foot in this Arrowhead country, and his charm and high spirits (to say nothing of his imagination!) are evident in these *Voyages* of his. Nor can I bear to leave behind the quaint journals of traders like Peter Pond, Macdonell, Hugh Faries, and Nicholas Garry, exact and enthralling accounts of early canoe trips. But books are far too bulky. I must be content with the notebook into which I've copied my favorite passages.

I've warned my family at home that they won't hear from us for three weeks. We'll probably be able to send them some word, Lee says, but since we may not have a chance, it is better for them not to expect letters.

Thursday, August 25th

We have started!

I did appreciate our train's thoughtfulness in leaving Duluth so early yesterday morning; I could not have waited another half-day.

In the early afternoon we disembarked at Winton. Quite unreasonably, I'd been taking it for granted that we would start out from a long pier by a summer inn, with gay launches about and bright flags flying, people promenading in smart sport clothes, so that I'd feel rather conspicuous and shabby in my corduroys and packsacks, before we escaped from sight.

So I felt relieved, though astonished, when we left the train, to find only a dingy country town. The single unusual sight was an Indian family boarding the train: a fat chief, three women in scarlet and orange, and a small Indian boy with a huge basket of blueberries. One of the women had a papoose strapped to her back, which rather surprised me. I thought that custom had vanished long ago.

Lee saw that our canoe came out of the baggage car safely, and we went up to the general store to collect our last supplies. I changed from my traveling things to my corduroy outfit in the attic storeroom, we left our civilized baggage there, and the storekeeper loaded us, our canoe, and packsacks into a truck, took us out, and dropped us along a country road. It all seemed very casual.

Beyond a russet barn, a lake of gentian blue shimmered bright down a grassy hill. We carried everything down to a sketchy dock, we put our canoe in the water, our packs and ourselves in the canoe, and started off.

It was as simple as that.

At first, as we swung out and dipped our paddles into liquid sapphire, the ghosts of the sawmills which used to be so busy here stood all about us. When we got beyond their ruin, and passed summer cottages and boathouses for an hour or more, it was like being on the water at home. This was a mild beginning for adventure.

But when we came to our first portage path, and I helped to unload the canoe, and took the shadowy way with a pack on my shoulders, I felt this was a new experience after all. I carried the clothes pack, Lee took the miscellaneous sack on his back and lifted the canoe — with the paddles lashed in — over his head, so that the yoke fitted to his shoulders. The second trip he took the food pack and blanket roll, while I carried the camera, field glasses, and other odds and ends. I liked tramping over the portage twice with loads; I liked the smell of hot pines and the curve of ferns, the glimpse of dazzling water ahead.

We went down the second lake. Lee settled the packs lower, to lessen wind resistance as well as to steady the canoe. By sunset we had landed on a scrap of peninsula, I had watched Lee cut down a leafy poplar for our first tent pole, and had cooked my first supper over a campfire. Afterward, as we sat on the rocks in the afterglow, a muskrat swam across the

18

duskiness — our first wild animal. I waved a benediction at him before I went to bed.

Before I left New York, I had wondered whether it would not seem a little desolate to sleep on the ground in a tent, and if the night noises would keep me awake and restless. Even Nicholas Garry's diary did not entirely reassure me. "Nor Ghosts, nor Rattlesnakes, nor Spiders," he said, comfortingly, "nothing can prevent the fatigued Voyageur from sleeping." I had only hoped that I would be as unperturbed.

But now, as I crept between the blankets, I was far too drowsy to realize I was sleeping out of doors for the first time in my life. I went to sleep without a thought for my surroundings.

But this morning, the white mist about us, the exultant laughter of the loons (Lee's favorite birds in this country), made me feel I was really in a different land.

I've just learned how to break camp. There are two inviolable rules.

First, to leave the camping place as
unscarred as possible. Every bit of litter must
be burned or carefully hidden, so that we haven't made the forest uglier
by our presence.

Second, and even more important, every spark of fire must be completely extinguished. To cause immense destruction or perhaps death, because we hadn't taken the trouble to carry another pail of water, or wait
an extra minute, would be horrible.

We are starting now on our first long day's voyage. It is a blue and
immaculate morning, with a quiet wind pacing along with us.

I insist that I should be initiated, as each new *voyageur* was on enter-
ing this country, by being sprinkled with a cedar bough, with appropriate

ceremony, even if we can't manage "a dozen of gunshots fired one after another in an Indian manner." But Lee says that since I haven't a trapping license I am not really a *voyageur*, only a *coureur de bois*. Or should it be *coureuse?*

The loons are flying above us, still laughing. I would like to laugh as jubilantly, at all the people who said I wouldn't like a canoe trip!

Late afternoon

Now we are in the true forest; no more cabins since we left the forest ranger's, where we got our Canadian fishing license, this noon. We have been following the international boundary marks, which trace the ancient canoe route of the Indians. This morning we landed on a sand beach in the United States, to go swimming in the green and orange water; so we decided we would make camp in Canada this afternoon.

What a way to travel — no trains to catch, no traffic to annoy us, no towns to reach by evening, no appointments to remember! We wander anywhere our whims take us, through these lakes and rivers.

Freedom surrounds us. We are finding more than peace here. This is an authentic and profound release from modern intricacies.

I caught the rhythm of paddling today, so that the paddle, the canoe, and I were all one. The monotony of the dip, the push, and the swing has a peculiar fascination after a while. But my shoulders and back are still remembering it.

Our camp tonight is under an enormous white pine, by rapids of dark green glass and snow. Norway pines darken the rocky hill. The ground is covered with blueberry plants, thick with blue lusters. It seems a crime to eat these berries of lapis lazuli, but when we discovered them we never thought of aesthetic scruples — we seized them with both hands.

I speak with such authority about the white and Norway pines, because I've just been learning, from shining examples on the shore, the differences between them. The white is the one with the beautiful horizontal

21

masses. Its three-sided needles, blue-green and
pliable, come in clusters of five, and its grayish bark
is rough and deeply grooved in old trees. The Norway is straight and tall
(though it cannot reach the height of the largest white pines) with a
reddish trunk. Its stiff dark green needles, flat on one side and rounded
on the other, come in clusters of two.

I've just been down the rocks picking up decorative pine cones for my
campfire. There was a runaway little kingfisher on a twig, pretending to
be an austere and steady fisherman. But he had his father's best white collar on, much too big for him — it came to his eyes — while his hair stuck
up straight with excitement and his tiny feet clutched the twig so ar-
dently I know he was inwardly overwhelmed by his venture.

Lee is fishing too. He has gone over to a narrow island to fish the rapids. Two packsacks lie inside the tent; the third one, with the food and cooking things, keeps me company here. We'll have pancakes and coffee tonight, fish perhaps, certainly blueberries.

Night

While Lee was across the rapids, he caught a ponderous pickerel, and also caught the fishhook in his hand. It came out docilely enough, thank heaven, but when he reached our shore he was bleeding all over the canoe and the rocks and moss, though he was too proud of his capture to notice it. At home I would probably have shrieked and swooned, but here, as there was no one to dash to my aid, I bandaged him up in such a coolly efficient manner that I stood in awed admiration of myself.

As I was serving supper on the rock, I remembered Garry's description of his table, and scrambled in the pack to get my notebook, so that I could read aloud to Lee:

"Our Dinner Table was a hard Rock, no Table Cloth could be cleaner and the surrounding Plants and beautiful Flowers sweetening the Board. Before us the Waterfall, wild romantic, bold. The River Winnipic here impeded by Mountainous Rocks appears to have found a Passage through the Rocks and these, as if still disputing the Power of Water, show their Heads, adding to the rude Wildness of the Scene, producing Whirlpools, Foam loud Noise, and chrystal Whiteness beautifully contrasted with the Black Pine."

It's just the same. What a chance this is, to see granite shores which haven't changed at all, in the three hundred years that have transformed Manhattan from a quiet coast to the most amazing city on earth! To step back in time, and see this country, as the first explorers saw it, as the Indians did when they were its conquerors! Here, one hundred years *is* but a day.

Lee liked the "Whirlpools, Foam loud Noise, and chrystal Whiteness" as much as I did, so I went on to read him Radisson's description of the moose — he calls it sometimes an Eland and sometimes an Oriniack.

"Most of the woods and forests are very thick, so that it was in some places as darke as in a cellar, by reason of the boughs of trees. The snow that falls, being very light, hath not the strength to stopp the eland, which is a mighty strong beast, much like a mule, having a tayle cutt off 2 or 3 or 4 thumbes long, the foot cloven like a stagge. He has a muzzle mighty bigge."

Here Radisson branches off to the "Buff" which "is a furious animal. One must have a care of him . . ." But surely he is talking of the moose again when he says,

"I have seene of their hornes that a man could not lift them from of the ground. They are branchy and flatt in the midle, of which the wild-man makes dishes that can well hold 3 quarts. These hornes fall off every yeare, and it's a thing impossible that they will grow againe."

How can I wait to see an Oriniack!

Friday

We had a sunny and strenuous day's canoeing, with many portages. One very long one, in the late morning, to avoid a series of rapids. The path was so constantly sunny, through small bushes, asters, and goldenrod, up and down hot little hills with rocks to stumble over, that two trips seemed unbearable. I tried to call up visions of La Vérendrye and his sons stalking along this path, of Radisson, debonair and blithe. But I could only picture them in snow or rain or gloom of night. I don't believe they could cope with heat either.

Lunch was on a small hot island under some very unsatisfactory jack pines. These are scrub pines and take all sorts of shapes; we've even seen several solitary ones trying to look like apple trees. How we would have appreciated one like that! But these were contrary creatures, too thin for shade. I felt like shaking shadows out of them.

By keeping our luncheon provisions (just picnic things, cheese crackers, chocolate, and raisins) in the top of the food pack, we don't need to unpack every noon. Simpler and simpler. So after lunching lightly

and making lemonade with our lemon powder, we allowed ourselves a short nap. Then on through the hot afternoon.

The rivers were like Peter Pond's favorites, "Verey Gental but Verey Sarpentine." And the lakes were motionless. But we weren't; we were hot and dripping. Who was it told me I'd freeze in this canoe country?

Then Lee decided to teach me to paddle and steer at the same time, and I was not a success. My exertions and Lee's hootings were becoming quite unbearable when, just after three, we turned north away from the international route, and found paradise.

In the first place, we came to a cliff and felt real shade for the first time since early morning. Here we drifted awhile, dipping our hands in the water, and cooling our vivid faces. Then we went on into three small circle lakes which lay, one after another, like strung sapphires.

The island we have chosen to camp on is in the second lake. The first is only half enchanted, but this is wholly so; and as for the third one, it is so bewitched you can't even talk there. I know; we've tried it.

Our own lake is decorated with big round green lily pads and small oval ones of rose and gold. The pine trees stand sedately around it, trailing their reflections in the rippled water, and a flock of little flapper ducks, too young to fly, had it for their own until we came.

Down a very zigzag path — for I was still steering — we came to our chosen island, and its long shadows looked very welcome after the sun's bright glare and Lee's admonitory one. Our tent is on the northern tip of the island. We look out past a great sweep of pine bough to the waters of our lake and the silent misty one beyond.

This is the moment, I think, when I've really given my heart to our canoe country, though I've been entranced with it from the first. But here its special quality of wild innocence touches me sharply and deeply.

I should very much like to live here forever. It's sorcery. It's not our world at all; it's another star.

26

This evening we set out to acquaint ourselves with our territories. Back to the first lake of the chain, where there were beaver houses to investigate. Then across our own lake again, laughing and talking nonsense.

But at the inlet to the third, we fell silent. If we didn't make a noise, Lee muttered, pretending he could talk if he wanted to, we might see a deer.

The water was without a ripple. Its candid ring was edged with tall bulrushes, spare dark whips exactly reflected. Great pines stood up around it in lovely broken lines, and down a narrow marsh we saw a great blue heron motionless in the tufted grass.

We slipped without a sound through the tranquillity. The rushes slanted above our heads as we floated by.

We came to the channel of an ethereal river, vanishing among the reeds. There was no breath of sound. Great white boulders gleamed here and there in the clear waterway. The rushes massed around us. Along silent curves we slid, on and on, until at last a small rapids rushed down from the black sanctuary of the forest.

Its foamy course broke the silence; we took a breath, and turned our canoe homeward.

It was dusk now, but a faint clear light still held. As we drifted back through the high reeds, great horizontal ripples came slowly toward us through the crystal water. It gave me the oddest sensation — our canoe seemed to be rising straight up into the twilight air. But that would not have been unnatural, after all, in this strange place.

We heard a great horned owl call, far away. Darkness was coming down the hills. In the pale water before me, an otter curved momentarily, and the silver wake of a beaver flashed, far down the other lake.

At the inlet, we could see our small white tent glimmering in the center of the island, in the center of the lake, in the center of the forest. Here was the center of the world.

Saturday

It's cool this morning. I'm writing this in a tall pine wood. Giant pines range up a long hill, with clean open spaces between the bronze trunks instead of all the undergrowth and ferns and twisted branches we usually have. Morning sunlight falls down to the matted needles in bars of brown sunniness and gold mist. The wind tastes fresh, pungent, and wild.

How utterly different this forest land is from the other two I've loved! Fontainebleau, a medieval dream forest (of course we saw it in April); the New Forest, the essence of England's beauty, where Robin Hood might appear down any glade. This country never knew a medieval time; it came straight from the primeval into today. And as for Robin Hood, I can't quite picture him scrambling over logs or hunting moose in a canoe.

We've been up the river. We portaged past the rapids — it seems so easy to portage when the baggage is home in camp! — and on up the stream. We found grassy banks, with spruce behind them, and then burned-over hills, bare and haunted. Giant trunks lay along the banks, their roots and branches distorted in the air. The river became so persistent in its stones and boulders that we could barely push through.

We met our first pileated woodpecker here, high on a charred pine. (At least, *he* was on the charred pine.) He is very shy and is found in the wildest places, so I was glad to have a chance to gaze at him.

He was a stunning bird, about twice as large as our red-headed woodpecker; black with a pattern of white on wings and neck, and a flashing red crest. He looked so powerful I longed to see him attack a tree, for he cuts and chisels like mad, hanging on by his feet and using his whole body for a hammer. Chips and strips of bark fly in every direction, and he sometimes rips off pieces a foot long.

30

But he didn't perform for me. He
went away instead, flashing the great spots
of white beneath his wings as he flew, and left
me lost in admiration.

Lee says the courtship dance of the pileated
woodpecker is most extraordinary. The male
and female meet on a treetop, spread their
pinions wide (they're between two and three
feet across) and hop and balance and bow to
each other. Sometimes they kiss or feed each
other, and then begin their posturing again.
What a strange spectacle it would be, against
the sky! Often they fly up and wheel in circles
through the air, with fluttering wings and
pointed crests, and then come down to dance
again on the branches. I wish I could see them.
I wonder if they look as joyful as the black and
white lapwings we saw tumbling down the sky
in England.

Saturday Evening

This afternoon we went down to the Painted Rocks and climbed the
cliff, to a lake that was lying obstinately on top of the hill, instead of at
the bottom where it belonged! We found a very jungle-y place where
something had been wallowing. And on the cliff edge were the most
enormous blueberries in the world. Hothouse blueberries, almost as big
as grapes.

Then, in the canoe, we floated under the Painted Rocks.

On the overhanging cliffs, Lee pointed out to me the vague outlines of
moose, in red pigment. The first explorers saw these too. In Macdonell's

journal he tells of some at Derraud's Rapids between Lake Huron and the Ottawa River:

"The figure of a man standing over an animal that lays under him, with a sun on one side and a moon on the other . . . A little farthur on is at least 16 figures of different animals standing promiscuously together on the face of a steep Rock . . . painted with some kind of Red Paint."

Above the drawings was a crack into which the Indians used to shoot their arrows. A friend of Lee's once climbed up and found arrowheads there.

It's threatening rain tonight, and Lee is making the tent snug, seeing that the wall canvas is tucked under the floor cloth on every side, and digging a shallow trench around us.

Sunday, August 28th

It did rain last night. It is raining today.

I woke in the night to the sound of rain pounding its tiny fists against the canvas so near our heads. I couldn't believe I was out in such a fragile shelter in the middle of a storm. Such frail walls to hold off such a bombardment. But our tent seemed to be intact and dry, so serenely I folded my hands and went to sleep again.

When I awoke this morning the lake was silver gray, and gray mist dimmed the forests. Our merganser ducks, feeling important, were steamboating like mad around the lake. Twenty-four of them in a proud little line, making reckless splatters in the rain.

We made a pygmy fire of pine cones and twigs, sheltering it between two stones in the tent opening. Just enough of a campfire for hot coffee. With it we ate ham and rye crisp and apricots, and watched from our refuge for ducks or deer. Only some Indians came past in a heavily laden canoe, bound, I suppose, for a reservation up on Lac la Croix.

I had to struggle against an idiotic pity for our canoe, lying on the shore, upside down and shining wet, in the plunging rain! I have become very fond of this companion of ours, which carries us along so resolutely. All the more because one is so thwarted in an affection for a canoe —there's nothing to do for it. If I could only give it a loose rein, or feed it hay or gasoline! But it is completely independent. I can only pat it slightly now and then.

Later it rained more gently, so we put on our raincoats and went out to fish. I decided that fishing in the rain is far more glamorous than fishing in the sun, for the lake was gray moire, the mistiness changed from gray to soft Madonna blue, and the distant islands had dimmed to phantoms of faint violet. The rain made a tiny patting sound on the lily leaves and on our hats.

An osprey circled over the lake searching for fish. Then he sat in the top of a pine and looked down meditatively into the water. *Le Penseur.* I don't know what he caught, but I caught four pike, a bass, and a water lily as lovely as an ivory carving.

33

It is now sitting in a tin cup under the dripping pine, looking as out of place as a duchess in a wheelbarrow.

Monday, August 29th

We arose at the hour of five this morning, to chase a moose we had heard in the night.

Never hear a cow moose in the night, when you don't know what it is! It is the most blood-freezing sound, a wild and wailing whoop, un-canny as Dracula. I heard it first at midnight. "Lee! What is that?"

"Well," he said thoughtfully, "it doesn't sound exactly like wolves!"

If *he* doesn't know what it is, I thought, after all his canoe trips!

"Lee," I said, after thinking wistfully of guns and revolvers, "Lee, where is the axe?"

"Down on the shore by the canoe."

And then that awful howl, much nearer this time. But there wasn't anything to be done and I went back to sleep. However, Lee, hearing it again before daylight, decided it was a lovelorn moose. So he woke me up and we started out to find it.

We couldn't see a thing beyond the rocks where the canoe lay. It was fantastic, launching the canoe into an immensity of fog; we were paddling in a white cloud. But to my relief we didn't fall through.

After a time we got the vaguest of shore lines; by then the lake was so thick with rushes that we slid along through them as if we were paddling in a grassy meadow. We found the mouth of the phantom river and went along, surprising a flock of black ducks and two great blue heron. There were no moose.

On our way back, a deer stirred in the grass along the shore. Lee paddled very gently toward her, while I found I couldn't manage my breath, to say nothing of the field glasses. As we drew near, Lee took only a stroke now and then when she lowered her head to eat, till at last we were in the reeds beside her. When we glided up close to the delicate

34

creature she gazed astonished. Then she whirled off among the upspringing birches.

I had wondered, I'll admit, if a three weeks' trip might not seem monotonous part of the time, in such a complete solitude. But I was wrong. Our life is as full here, for the time being, as it is in New York, with all its companions from every part of the world, its great art and music, its floodtides of ideas.

For every second, every inch, of this experience is filled with utter harmony. We take our way wherever we like; the animals and birds are as good company as one could ask; and if we tried we couldn't find an unsightly spot or a jarring note.

No despairs are here. And no man-made dangers. The bright eyes of the beasts need only look for their natural enemies, and we ourselves can forget all the world's turmoils and antagonisms. This absolute freedom gives every hour an intense lucidity.

Tuesday

We broke camp yesterday morning, breaking our hearts as well, as we left our circle lakes behind us. I couldn't have left if it had been as ethereal as usual, but it was a dull and forbidding morning, with clouds of iron ranging low. After we were well away, however, the day forgot its sullenness.

All day long we came west through the intricacies of Crooked Lake. Lovely river ways, wide stretches of cornflower water, studded islands; shores ranging from great bare hills just touched with delicate green by the young birches and poplars to massive tangled forest.

This was a day with people in it. First, in the morning, we met two boys from St. Paul, going out. They offered to take our mail, so the two canoes clung together for a while, in mid-lake, while Lee talked to the boys about their experiences and I scribbled an enthusiastic letter to the family.

Then at noon, as we passed a low island with a camp on it, we saw a lone man dancing and leaping and shouting wildly. He wasn't in pain, nor were his shouts ecstasy; they were just yells.

In the twilight this would have been quite eerie; even at noon it was grotesque enough — that tousled figure, leaping in the sun.

We didn't know whether he was drunk, or touched by the silence of this country. We had a Chicago friend, a man who had always lived in cities, who came here for an outing but went out the second day. He said he couldn't stand the feeling that there wasn't anyone beyond a hill. Sometimes, they say, when a ranger is here alone for months, he goes slightly mad from the solitary unconfinement.

So, as the dancer didn't call to us for help, I was glad to hurry past this island.

We ate our lunch farther along, with me keeping a wary eye out for a delirious canoe. Much to Lee's amusement, the wretch.

The afternoon freshened, with a gusty wind and high-piled clouds. At first we had many islands, but later in the afternoon we came to the western end of the lake, which was almost a "traverse," as the *voyageurs* called a wide stretch of water. The waves grew choppy enough to make it quite exciting. We lurched and shipped water until I had to bail, for the first time in our journey. I was glad Lee had had so much experience in canoeing.

Lee remembered a very beautiful point near the Curtain Falls, but as we approached it we could see two white tents in among its pines. Baffled — why were *people* around here, anyway? — we went past almost to the falls and found a camp site on a small stony bay, with drooping jack pines on it and a heavy forest behind.

Here we are two Gullivers in Lilliput. We have a great stir of wild life around us, in an extremely small way. Chipmunks by the score gallop around, mad with curiosity. Chickadees swarm in the pines, right side up or upside down, it doesn't seem to matter; their *dee-dee-dee*'s are con-

stant. Starring the camp are dragonflies of
every kind, bronze ones, gigantic emerald ones
almost as big as the chickadees, small ones of
gossamer blue, which are my special favorites.

And when I went down the shore to get driftwood, I ran into a migration of yellow warblers, hundreds of them, flicking in and out of the foliage like yellow sparks.

I sat down on a ledge to watch them. My hand against the harsh surface made me think of the stones themselves.

The rock formation of this whole country, I read somewhere, is part of the great Canadian Shield, so called because its surface of more than a million square miles, surrounding Hudson Bay on three sides and coming down into the United States at this point, is in the shape of a vast shield. This shield is of pre-Cambrian rocks, the oldest on the crust of the earth. From 48,000,000 to 1,710,000,000 years old! Those figures made a deep impression.

I looked back to those primordial ages, with the sundered stone around me — the stone that is the most ancient thing that we can see or touch in our world. The vastness of this shield and its antiquity was overwhelming me, when the *chee*-ing of the warblers made me turn back to them. Their evanescent yellow feathers flitted as gaily as ever through the cobweb green. I picked up my firewood and went home.

We had our supper on the rocks by the water, with impulsive chipmunks crowding us. One especially, dashing in and out of woodpecker holes like a miniature clown, distracted me terribly from my cooking. After supper I began to wash my dishes, but there was an afterglow of such luminous peach-gold that we left the dishes unregarded on the shore. Floating off into the spacious evening, without a ripple in the clear light above or below us, we set out to see Curtain Falls.

The falls, rough and dangerous, hypnotized me. The black smoothness of the water, just before it curved over the falls, was savagely elemental. We stayed till dark watching it, the spray and the green underswing; listening to the loons call.

When we got back to our point, we still had the Lilliputians about. Two tiny wood mice came out to clear away our crumbs. They were comic things, with their big eyes and round fuzzy ears and bits of whiskers. I felt quite guilty, liking them so much, when I shriek at house mice.

But I was in a liking mood. I even enjoyed washing my dishes, with the black night all about and stars in my rinsing water.

We saw the red sun come up this morning, through white mist. Our customary breakfast, blueberries, flapjacks, bacon, and coffee, tasted unusually good out on our rocks, even though the chipmunks chanted crossly at us because there were no prune seeds. After breakfast we went to Roland Lake portage to find a moose swamp Lee remembered. We found the swamp but no moose.

Only more loons. But they repaid us. I had never before been near enough to see how they run along the water's surface before they fly, and their spattering strides across the lake amused me enormously. Nor had I known before that they can vary their specific gravity at will, so that they float either with their spotted black and white bodies showing or with just the sleek black heads and striped necks above water.

We made a game of timing their long dives under water — they are magnificent submarines — and seeing who could guess how long they would stay submerged. One stayed under four minutes and a half — he was our champion. But they have been known to stay as long as eight minutes.

I hadn't realized before that loons are strictly water birds. They can barely hobble on land, though they make such swift runs on the lakes. And their flying seems to be done under water as well as in the air, for they use their wings as well as their feet in their long dives. They are all mixed up about locomotion. I turn giddy thinking of them, soaring in reverse, with fish about them.

Lee says they have many calls. The common laughing call, *hoo-hoo-hoo-hoo*, and the night call we have heard. Then there is a storm call, and what is known as the "silly song," as well as shorter notes.

Coming back, we met the people who are camping on the point. There were two canoes, a couple in one, in the other a guide and a fat man who, believe it if you can, wore a big white life preserver! He was

quite complacent about it, but the red-headed guide looked as shamefaced as a small boy does when a doll is forced upon him.

Wednesday, August 31st

These voyaging days are translucent with joy. When we start out in the morning, the earth has such a before-Eden look that it seems a shame to shake the dew from the blueberries or strike our paddles into the sleeping water. Thrusting on into sun-filled channels; drifting into green-needled embrasures where chickadees are buoyant; landing on a beach to bathe and to read the overnight paw prints — it is all intoxicating.

Now we have left the smooth pine slopes and the great bare hills of stone. We have come to rugged shores, ancient pines, and huge creviced rocks, rich in tone, padded deep with hoary moss and gray-green lichens. When the lakes are calm, they reflect the most glowing colors, dark wines and purples and crimsons, deep blues and greens, that we haven't noticed on the banks.

Only after we have seen the pure colors in the water do we look up and distinguish them in the tree trunks and cliffs, where we have seen only browns and greens because we weren't expecting anything else. An artist once told me that if you really want to see the color of a landscape you should stand on your head. This of course is practically the same thing.

We are camping on a jagged island in Lac la Croix.

Until now I have been very amenable about our camps. I've liked to go along and never know when Lee would say, "Why not camp here?"

But that is changed. Yesterday on the Curtain Falls portage — by the way, have I said how deeply I approve of portages? After miles of sunny waters, to have a chance to use your legs instead of your arms for propulsion, to plunge into a crisp, shadowed path, sundering ferns and bushes, brushing spiced boughs, a turquoise lake behind, unknown water ahead, feet clinking on the stones! In our doubled trips across, I never get quite

44

used to leaving half of all our worldly
goods sitting unprotected on the rocks. Nor can
I ever take for granted the wood fragrance, so different
from the smell of the air on the lakes. I have pine scent inextricably mixed
with portages now; one will always make me remember the other.

As I was saying, on this portage we met a couple who had been fishing
for deep lake trout. The four of us sat down by the black curves and foam
white of the rapids and talked, mostly about trout. However, Mrs. Morse
did mention casually that they had seen no moose this year but that
wolves seemed unusually prevalent, and so they had preferred to camp on
islands.

So now I prefer to camp on islands too.

I can't help it. Lee teases me, and I know it's foolish, that the wolves
can swim if they're really hungry, that they only get ravenous in winter,

and that even in winter it is extremely doubtful that they ever attack man. But still Mrs. Morse's words reverberate in the air. And after all, why *not* camp on islands?

They're much more interesting than mainlands, which run on and on in an aimless sort of way. Each island we meet has an individuality of its own, serene or careless or aloof. We saw an innocently wanton one clad in nothing but two daisy plants.

Our present island was bequeathed to us by the Morses.

It's just beyond Bottle Portage. It may be the one where Macdonell "Killed a cub Bear and slept in sight of the Mai." The mai was a lobstick or maypole, a favorite landmark of the *voyageur*, made by cutting away most of the branches of a tall tree. I like to think what welcome signs they must have been, just as the international boundary markers are hailed by us with joy.

This is an island with an escarpment, rather high and harsh, around three sides. To the west we have a small harbor, a semicircle of flat clean-washed stones. The center has an open space for our tent, the rest is inexorably wooded, and the thick dark moss under the trees is wonderful to walk on barefoot.

How much more sensitive we are to feeling in this primitive environment! In fact, all five senses are much more wide awake. Of course, one would expect seeing and hearing to be more enjoyable here, since there are only pleasant sights and sounds. And taste is proverbially keener out of doors.

But how much more I notice the touch of things! The smooth paddle in my hand, the shock of cold water on my face, the texture of rough sticks and pine cones when I pick up firewood. The slimness of pine needles in my fingers, the springy turf or hard granite when I step.

And the increased keenness in the sense of smell. I wish we had a better word for *smell* — one that didn't suggest a disagreeable sensation! *Scent, fragrance, odor,* they are all too sweet, too flowery. No, *smell* is

46

what I mean, the different way that early morning smells, and twilight. The changes one forest path can give you as you walk along, the scent of wet green leaves, and dried brown ones, of mushrooms, and crushed grass. . . .

Last night it was cold. There was a hint of a new moon in the apple-green sky, and a wind in the pines all night long. Snug in my blankets, I could imagine that the branches above us still held faint echoes of war drums, or the songs of the *voyageurs:*

> *"Quand j'étais chez mon Père,*
> *Petite Janeton,*
> *Il m'envoyait à la fontaine*
> *Pour pêcher du poisson.*
> *La Violette Dandon, oh!*
> *La Violette dandé. . . ."*

But it's time to get breakfast. Lee has gone over to the other side of the island to see whether a certain eagle is golden or only bald, and I've been scribbling, far too long.

Lee will expect flapjacks when he gets back. I'm an expert flapjack-maker by now, for our bread is all gone. Lee is better at the actual flap, however, for when I do it, the flapjack, instead of turning the customary mild summersault, soars so high that it is quite cold by the time it comes down.

I cook fish very well now; my boiled beans with bacon and my outdoor coffee are delicious. The only things I cannot cook are the dried peas. I have boiled some for three days, carrying them hope-fully along with us, setting them on a fire the minute we stop, and still they rattle stubbornly when the water bubbles. I mean to give them to this chipmunk who thinks he helps me cook. He is the smallest one I have ever seen, and the most engaging. And I'm afraid he knows very well that he is, for he poses outrageously. Now he is sitting on the very tip of a dead cedar bough, eating a prune seed, and only glancing at me fleetingly over his minute shoulder. Sublimely preoccupied!

48

We were marooned yesterday on a sand beach. We went to see some more painted rocks, even more interesting than the first cliff, with moose and men in war canoes and the prints of many hands, all in bright red.

These paintings make the primitive red man seem startlingly alive, much more so than seeing modern Indian culture ever has. Especially these prints of hands. Real hands . . . I had a ghostly feeling.

While Lee was trying to photograph the paintings the wind had streamed down against us harder and harder. White plumes filled the lake till Lee thought it was hazardous to attempt to passage back to the island.

So we scurried on, around a more or less sheltered shore, and found a short sand beach between two vertical cliffs. It was a mere dune between the lake and a swamp beyond, but we took refuge there.

Climbing up ponderable rocks of gray and green and orange to a small cave garlanded with vines, we ate a lunch of cheese and chocolate, which Lee happened to have, luckily, in his pocket. Below us the waves pounded against the sand.

Now, as we sat in our cave, sheltered from the strong gusts, a whole family of moose birds gathered around us, looking at us with friendly eyes, cocking their black-capped heads inquisitively.

This fluffy gray bird is a jay, the Canada jay, also called the camp robber and Whisky Jack, the last derived from his Indian name, Wis-ka-tjon. He seems to have no fear of man at all, though he chooses to live in the wild woods instead of around settlements. I had been wanting to see a moose bird, having heard so many tales of his brazenness and robberies.

But I decided today that he is misjudged.

Crows are crafty and clever thieves, taking an ironic pride in their knavery. But the moose bird is so wide-eyed and innocent—I can't believe he thinks he is a robber at all; he just borrows things, feeling sure you won't mind, since he is a friend of yours.

These particular birds sat near us companionably. After a little, Lee set out a crumb of cheese and a crumb of chocolate on the rim of the ledge. Both were snatched up at once. Before long the family was diving and dipping past us, catching slivers of chocolate or cheese or silver paper from our fingers, and perching along the vines. We enjoyed this entertaining in a cave!

After our refreshments had vanished, our guests did too, and we climbed down and explored the hill east of the swamp, till a red squirrel, singing a real little melody up in a tree, saw us and began to scold instead. Really, the animals are as stern with us as they were with Alice in Wonderland. We ruefully made our way back to the beach.

I sat down on the sand and thought delightedly of being reprimanded by a squirrel. I began to realize that one of the deepest joys of this vacation, which I had scarcely been conscious of, is the nature of our social

contacts. So clear, so direct — a squirrel's dislike, the wordless friendship with the jays, the comedy offered by two ants with a flag of dried beef, the awe an ancient pine awakes. After the complicated stresses and emotions a metropolitan day engenders, gatherings where intricate attractions and repulsions web the air, confidences given, advices asked for unsolvable problems, faces in the subway with expressions that tear one's heart . . . Of course one wouldn't want to escape the complex demands forever. But for a breathing space — what a release!

While Lee began a color sketch of the cliff, I lay in the half-shade of tall grass, by a twisted ash tree. When I pillowed my head on my arm I could look along the honey-colored pebbles into a medley of wild-rose briars. Swept by the strong south wind, lulled by the assault of the waves against the sand, I remembered drowsily the first time I ever discovered that poetry had the power to give me cold tingles up and down my back. I could hear the golden voice of our tall young English teacher as clearly as I had when I was thirteen:

> *"And answer made the bold Sir Bedivere:*
> *I heard the ripple washing in the reeds,*
> *And the wild water lapping on the crag. . . .*
>
> *I heard the water lapping on the crag,*
> *And the long ripple washing in the reeds."*

With that murmur in my mind I drifted off to sleep.

When I woke, the wind was more boisterous than ever, and the waves were storming in, so I went wading down the shore. Of course I got drenched, but it didn't matter; I simply went in swimming. It was glorious! The lake glittered darkly blue, the pines were emerald sequins flashing in the wind. Long tangles of water grass wavered in gold-brown streamers about me, and then the brilliant sand shone clear again through the surge. The waves, rough as half-grown puppies, played about me, tossing me over, pushing me back to land.

52

At sunset the wind lessened, and we came back to our island camp.

By the way, Lac la Croix seems to have a reputation for marooning travelers. I have a note from Hugh Faries' diary:

Friday, August 17, 1804

"Embarked this morning and proceeded down to Lake Lacroix, but it blew such a strong head wind, that we did not go far forward. . . . Strong wind and clear weather. [Just like today.]"

Saturday, August 18

"Early this morning we proceeded to the little portage La croix tho' it blew very hard a head. at 1 oclock the men went down with a demie charge to the Pines. they return'd at Sunset having damaged their canoes."

Sunday, September 4th

We decided to come exploring down the Bear Trap River. It is the most unfrequented place that Lee can think of, near by, and he hopes we may find moose. Deer we have seen often, though I've only mentioned one — I *can't* seem to get everything in — but all these days and not one moose has appeared. Lee is quite desperate.

The forests were more patrician than usual this morning. Narrow gold diagonals fell through the green-towered ramparts, and the air was cool and touched with fragrance. The water rippled clearly, darkly; outside a shadowy cove the sky to the west bloomed with pale clouds of lavender and faint purple and that creamy fire opals have. I needed some ritual to follow, an orison of worship.

Today we saw our first bear! Lee made me jump by laughing suddenly; he saw it slip from the bluff it was climbing. It fell into the water with a splash, surprising itself and Lee enormously. I was only in time to see a dark shape scramble up the bank, and later, by paddling hard, we had a glimpse of its grotesque silhouette against the skyline for a moment. Lee said that bears will not condescend to hurry if they know you are watching them, but they make up for it as soon as they think they're out of sight.

Later in the morning a gale came up again while we were crossing Iron Lake. The water turned a deep violet, the waves were urgent and white capped. We had to struggle violently to make headway; it was fun, but it was a real combat. Cloud shadows and flashes of sun whirled by us, as we dug our paddles furiously into the surging assault.

"I'll quarter against the wind," Lee shouted to me. "If I drive straight into it, the waves are too close together. We hit too hard."

I was completely exhausted by the time we finally rounded a rugged point and came to smooth, washed shores of pale ivory that were banked by sooty jack pines in close thickets. Here we discovered the mouth of Bear Trap River.

This was a hidden river of abrupt turns and many boulders; remote and casual, it may not have been traversed for many years. A weight of sun lay on its low shores; reeds and rushes and yellow pond lilies, black ducks, blue herons, and bluer kingfishers bedecked it lavishly.

We had lost the wind. It was midsummer and midnoon. We made our way slowly up the river, until we came to a portage. Here was simply

54

an immense face of cliff, seemingly unscalable, blocking the river, which disappeared in an offhand manner.

Even if it hadn't been remorselessly hot, I was sleepy from fighting the waves all morning. I assembled a modest lunch, though untying the strings of the bag seemed an impossible task. "Hurray," I said to myself, as I gazed at the cliff, "that's stopped us. I can have a nap."

But Lee, fascinated beyond words by the disappearance of the river, was enthusiastic about climbing over the cliff to see what we'd find.

I loathed the idea! I felt fuzzy in my knees, my face was a scarlet flare, and I knew I could never drag myself over the half-mile portage the map promised.

Before I could summon energy to express my violent disapproval, Lee was scrambling up the sheer rock with the canoe balanced on his head; so rebelliously I scrambled too.

We reached the top breathless, and I was allowed to lead the way along a lost path in dense forest. Outwardly a guide, but inwardly a whole mutiny. I hated this path as vehemently as I had loved all our other portages.

Nobody had come here for a long time, we could tell. But there were moose and bear tracks, and I had to scrabble through low branches and tangled places, where I couldn't see what I was going to meet.

I kept stumbling and stubbing my toes. I don't know why I always stub my toes when I am cross; it's one of the minor mysteries of life.

We crossed the portage at last and met the river again. It went placidly on, with grass bogs on either side—a perfect place for moose, Lee was sure. The sun was too hot for me even to mention what I knew perfectly well: there wouldn't be any moose.

There weren't any moose. Nothing alive appeared on that river, except a very drowsy turtle on a rock.

We toiled on down the river, until we came to a place where beavers had been gnawing down trees with industrious teeth and building a super-

56

solid dam. Even to contemplate the enormous amount of labor they had lavished on it made me feel shattered. Infuriating, haggard, short-winded beasts beavers must be, I thought, working like that. They'd be proud of themselves, too, for being all worn out. I disliked them heartily. But at least their dam stopped our expedition.

When we had dragged ourselves back to the luggage and embarked again, Lee was not long in finding a place to camp. He indicated a rocky point.

"Splendid to watch for moose here."

But I felt supremely indifferent to moose, and it was a very small point. The next possible place, a jack pine wood, I refused too; it was too closely overgrown. The third discovery was a bare rock slope with a little thicket, and black forest beyond.

"There!" said Lee triumphantly.

"It isn't an island," I murmured.

"Of course it is. See that marsh — it probably leads around to the river again." He looked so hot, poor lamb, that I couldn't insist on more paddling. I accepted the place as a possible island, and we landed here.

Lee made me lie down in the shade of a scraggy pine, while he made camp. I was almost asleep when he came gaily along, to show me that a bear had been overturning rocks in search of ants, just by our tent. Like Queen Victoria, I was *not* amused. What if it comes back for an ant it has overlooked?

This really is a magnificent view, with the river curving widely on one side, and a great grass marsh on the other. But it's aloof and alien to me; this isn't an intimate place. I'm not a part of it as I've been in our other camps. I don't want to stay here longer than one night.

September 5th

Today has been superb! Such sudden changes! And we've had a Noah's Ark of animals all day long.

59

It started badly. When we woke it was still hot and sultry, with a heavy feeling in the air. Forest-fire weather, Lee said, and we had breakfast down by the water, to be especially careful. A dismal breakfast in the sun, with the flapjacks gummy, cold coffee, and no fruit. For I'd forgotten to stew any of the dried fruits and bears have eaten the blueberries from this slope. Also, I spilled the prepared milk. And I felt disgruntled because the management had furnished no sand to scour my skillet, nor any soft thick grass to clear the dishes with.

Never mind. We went off to investigate the eastern swamp, which had an evasive fascination. Rivulets filtered through the slipping grass. Strange plants swayed in the shadowy greenness under our paddles. Little three-petaled flowers, frail as apple blossoms, floated awry in the swamp pools, where tenuous shapes wavered and dissolved. It was a sliding place, without validity.

But a west wind came up, and the air lightened. We found a small stream which led us to a hidden pond. Peering through the ice-green poplars, we discovered six deer bathing in the water! Like nymphs they looked, careless and unafraid. We watched them with delight until a splendid buck suddenly appeared on the far shore. Just for a glancing moment; then he caught our scent, and so we lost them all.

We started back in high spirits, with a kingfisher darting like a blue arrow ahead of us. Then I heard a noise. Like something crying.

"Lee, what is it?"

He listened. "It might be a bear cub."

It was a porcupine, up in a cedar tree, with its head between its paws, crying and crying.

One couldn't comfort a porcupine, but I got out on the bank to see it, and caught sight of another one, climbing a tall poplar. Hand over hand he went, like a man, and then swung hilariously on a high branch in the wind.

As we came back toward camp, Lee saw still another, walking around

60

our tent, the rascal. We were deluged with porcupines. When we reached the tent, we chased the intruder up a tree, and Lee threw my hat at him.

"Why, Lee!" I cried.

However, when I rescued the hat, it was skewered with several of the quills, which come out so easily whenever anything brushes against a porcupine, and so I could examine the needle point and the myriad barbs along each quill.

The fourth creature appeared down among the lily pads, swimming absurdly with both paws at once. I'd never heard of porcupines in the water, and I didn't expect it of them. Porcupines are so *dry* — it's like seeing a cactus take to swimming. But it seems the quills are slim tubes of air and buoy them up like water wings.

All afternoon was swift with clouds. The wind grew damp with coming rain, while a menace of navy blue piled up in the west.

Lee decided he saw a deer at the end of the bay, and if we slipped down along the grassy bank we would be quite close to her. She was looking so intently across the inlet that she didn't see us until we were within a canoe's length. Then off she went in a tremendous bound.

Then we saw why she had been gazing so steadily. Her spotted fawn had balked on the other bank. It looked at us with great soft eyes. We knew each other intimately, for one moment, before it disappeared.

As we came out into Bear Trap River again, it began to rain. At the same moment, "Moose!" Lee exclaimed.

I caught a glimpse of something brown downstream. Then it disappeared behind an outcrop of rock. What did rain matter when we could realize our ambition at last? We tore downstream. There it was. A cow moose in the water.

62

I stopped paddling; I was too excited not to splash. Then suddenly, beyond her we caught sight of a bull moose!

Two great prehistoric creatures in front of us, like the monsters you see in dreams.

We came closer and closer to them. Till I thought we were quite close enough, and began to talk. Loud enough to be noticed, I hoped.

For moose think very slowly, and they might have been muddle-headed enough to make a wrong turn and plunge into the canoe instead of away from it, if they were very suddenly surprised. Lee is almost too expert at creeping up on creatures.

When they finally did see us, they didn't believe in us. They gazed incredulously as we edged nearer. Then at last they splashed madly through the shallows away from us. Up the bank they went, breaking into the rocking trot I had been afraid I'd never see, and then we caught a last glimpse of them against the hill, between yellowing poplars.

We went home in triumph. Through a thunderstorm and a sunset, both at once, a sight most weirdly glorious.

A wild magenta light on the hills, the river in deep purple shadow, a blaze of flame color lighting the thunderheads above us, while jagged lightning, electric blue, zigzagged everywhere. It was like the Doré pictures in our *Paradise Lost*.

Especially when two fallen angels came coasting down the wind into the swamp. This was almost too much! When they settled down and transformed themselves into great blue herons, I felt greatly relieved.

Tuesday, September 6th

Of course it had to be last night, just after I had seen what mammoth creatures moose are! One came along in the middle of the night, took fright at our tent, and pounded off through the woods like a runaway locomotive. Such crashes from an Oriniack! I'm quite sure now I'd rather see than hear one.

64

I lay awake a long while, looking out at the dark, feeling that over-mastering awe of the black night and its terrors which is our inheritance from savage ancestors.

But I want the alarums as well as the excursions; I wouldn't want to miss the discords of these wild fastnesses.

We broke camp early this morning and fished on our way down the river, which was held captive in nets of white fog. I caught three bass, and we watched a mink wander along the shore, like a country gentleman out for a stroll.

We came out into the wide lake again. There was never a morning so completely flawless. Sky-blue water, wide shores backed by the dim lilac of pine ranges, great cloud foams of white and lavender piled up far behind them. Yet shore and clouds, great as they were, only a narrow strip between the pure blue above and below. When these big lakes are still—do you remember, when you were small, they filled a glass of water full for you, and then put on one more drop, so that the water stood up over the edge of the glass? These lakes seem overfull of beauty, like that, and sometimes I can hardly bear it.

September 7th

This is, I think, the most perfect camp of all. How can I say that, when they are all so different? When our three sapphire lakes were so especially glamorous? But that was a misted fairytale place. This is a clear carved design—true poetry.

It is so savagely sweet here; a pagan loveliness—Grecian paganism, untouched and pure. With all its wildness you would never be afraid.

Yesterday we meant to explore the bays on Lac la Croix. But on a small wild-rice bay there was a tantalizing portage to Lake McAree, and we found ourselves over here.

In the afternoon, I saw an Elysian island ahead of us and begged for it. There seemed no place to land, but it looked so mysteriously perfect

66

we went all around it, and found at last a secluded horseshoe to the north, where we could push in between fallen trees and water plants.

This island seemed never to have had anyone set foot on it. A most ancient and primeval place, all deep shadows and thick green moss and queer tall boulders. No wide sunny spaces, only bits of gold. Dark hollows filled with densely matted pine needles and vine tangles, doubled twisted trees leaning low over the water. There was no place to camp at all. But we felt held here, like Rat and Mole from *The Wind in the Willows*; we expected to hear the mighty Piper at any moment.

A little farther on we found a sunnier island, and another darker one, with a small and shimmering bay between. As we came into it, six mallard ducks were swimming there. They flew up as we came close, and went skimming around us and off over the trees.

As we went on, a single duck, flying up from the woods, went south and then came circling back. This was the mother duck, Lee was sure, and her children had already disappeared.

On through a narrow channel with a clean pine wood on the east shore, and around the corner we found a lily pond, peaceful and silvered; then we went past a point to a wide blue lake again. We didn't need to see any more. We came back through the inlet, and after hesitating between the clear pine wood and the sunlit island, we somehow chose the island.

When we landed, the great pine trunks were gilded with light, and ferns and mats of blueberries were enameled mosaics, gold, green-gold, and green-blue. There was a breath of scented wind, and then we heard a hermit thrush singing, the first one we have heard in our canoe country. That most haunting gold-dark song, golden with realized rapture, dark with unrealized grief — I shall never hear it again without longing for this place.

Lee made our camp above a ledge of rocks, in the midst of treetops. It was the hottest middle of the afternoon and I lay on my back in gray moss, soft and thick, in the shadow of the widest pine, and began a poem,

68

When the blue light comes
Through the great pine wood,
Clear and unblown
As blue light should —

while Lee chopped down trees with reckless enjoyment, and the mother duck flew wildly over the island, calling for her children.

When it was cooler and long shadows flung themselves down the hill, I cooked supper, while Lee cleaned the fish I had caught on the way down. I picked blueberries by the bush; it's quicker that way, and they make an exotic centerpiece, with the luminous berries, exquisite as flowers, and the pointed leaves now turned to crimson lacquer.

I had my most attractive place for camp cooking. A crack down the rocks for my fireplace, the flat top of the stony ledge for my table, and glimpses through interlaced boughs, over islands and golden water. Lee chopped a path down through the ash trees to the east shore, a little vista through green leaves, down to green ripples and slim reeds.

I was so enchanted with our home that I made a blueberry shortcake for supper, the first baking I've tried, using sweetened biscuit dough for the cake and the largest of my covered pots for an oven. It was a flagrant triumph.

As we ate supper we could see the blue night coming up the eastern sky. Blue night over there, and it was approaching us, step by step. I had never seen it come so unmistakably. It grew darker, and the small moon brightened. The shores and islands became black blots, and the moon began to make a faint rainbow path on the lake.

This half-moon made everything around us more solitary. I suppose because I've watched just such a moon so often at home. The island felt *farther away* than any place I've ever been.

Lee and I sat on the cliff's edge. Our duck came swimming around the island, from moonlight to dark shadow, still calling her lost children. She was so small a figure in the night, and she wasn't calling frantically now, but in a subdued way, reassuringly and tenderly.

When at last the mosquitoes drove us into our tent, there was still a view, through the netting, of black branches and a great emerald star.

Wild clouds, too, that grew wilder and heavier, till a terrific storm broke in the west. The lightning and thunder became almost continuous and the wind whooped in the trees. Lee got really worried about the tent's blowing away.

"Shall we pack everything?" he said. "Though if the tent goes it will be so tragic that all the little things might as well blow away too!"

We grew more and more hilarious as the wind blew harder and harder, and I laughed so at Lee's trying to hold on to three corners of the tent at once, dashing around like one of our chipmunks, that I could hardly hold the one corner I was responsible for.

We even made up songs about the tent, hoping it would be flattered enough to stay with us, and from that we progressed to all the old songs we'd ever known. It must have been surprising to the owls to hear

> *"Steamboat Bill, steaming down the Mississippi,*
> *Tryin' to break the record of the Robert E. Lee!"*

coming from an unsteady small tent, rocking on a rockbound shore, in the middle of a thunderstorm and the middle of the night.

September 9th

Ten days now since we've seen any human beings. It's quite a record. I haven't missed them at all.

This morning was washday. Down the path Lee had cleared, I carried my laundry to the jade-green pool shielded by lemon-scented bushes. Blackberry vines curled near. Some delicate dry grasses of pale cream

71

stood against the brilliant water. I splashed and rubbed my clothes on the stones and felt very archaic.

Spreading my array on the bushes to dry, I retreated to the pine shade. Here the moss was soft and brightly green, and I lay full length in it. So I discovered its flowers.

Flowers of the moss. I'd like to make a diminutive study of them. Shallow cups of pale green, bright scarlet tips enameled on green stems, tarnished silver discs. Coral dots, tawny seed pods high on slender threads, brown-petaled cups, gold points, rose points, gray-green trumpets. There is a deep gray moss like masses of tiny shrubs, a green velvet that covers stones as smoothly as upholstery, a pale green lichen like minute oak leaves. All these atoms are so *sturdy* in their miniature loveliness. I want to keep them.

This afternoon we came over to the ancient island. I am drifting around in the canoe, while Lee has gone ashore to sketch.

I'm in the bottom of the canoe, lying back against our coats. It's very still. Just a little lapping of the water on the stone near me — that's the only sound. Now and then I can hear Lee crashing somewhere on the island.

Such deep gloom up through the trees! Down here there are water plants whose graceful curled leaves start deep in the brown water, and reeds whose slender jointed stems sway high above the flat lily pads. Long swaths of grass lie on the liquid surface in irregular circles. Over the water a Norway pine swoops down; its lovely horizontal branches, its blue-green needles and rough twigs are reflected sharply. There are tiny warblers flying all through it, like truant piano notes. I'm so happy I can almost fly too.

We have been down to the rapids fishing. I laughed till I cried down there; any whoops the loons made were nothing to mine. As I stepped out of the canoe the rock was slippery and my foot slid into the water. Lee has been training me, ever since we started, in the proper way to enter

72

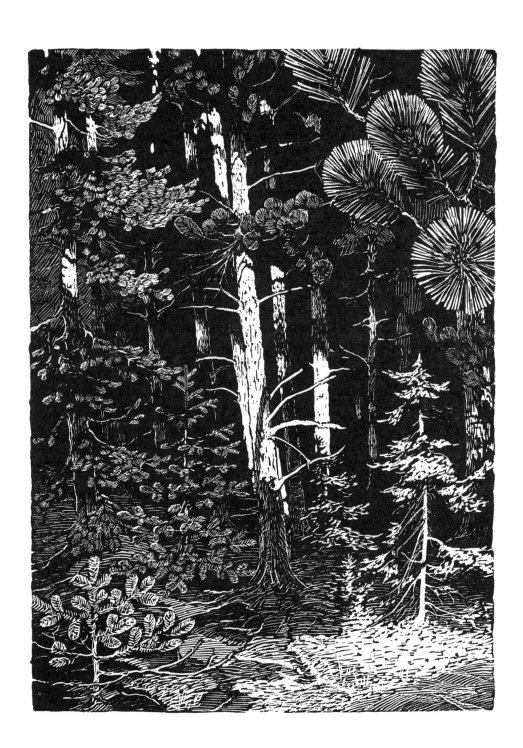

and leave a canoe, so now he said reprovingly, "No sense in that!" Then *he* stepped steadily out, on the same treacherous stone, and went, *zipp,* down on his back in the lake. I never saw such an amazed expression. "No sense in that, Lee!" I said sternly.

September 10th

The sunset yesterday was Blake's "eternity in an hour." Great bubbles of clouds, cream and soft fire and amethyst, floating over all the world, in a sky so boundless that the world was only a small, dimmer bubble itself. When I lay back against the rocks, and looked up into the intense soft blue, with great circles of pink and rose and soft lilac gleaming there, I was transformed from an earth creature into an airy one.

Feeling so light in spirit, I went canoeing. Lee remained lazily on shore, but I set out alone without a qualm. Only, when I got out into the lake and gusts of wind assailed me, I realized suddenly that it had been absolutely calm on the former occasions when I had been sole navigator. And then I had had a load to steady the canoe. Now it was empty-headed and as hard to control as most empty-headed people are. Its bow rose defiantly in the air. I couldn't manage to keep any direction. I bobbed around like a circus horse.

Lee began to shout from the shore, but his advice was mostly blown away. I felt as frantic as I do when I'm talking excitedly over the telephone and the family keeps calling additions and contradictions from the next room! In trying to follow the remnants of counsel which came to me, and to control my canoe and my laughter, I somehow got a violent cramp in my right hand.

Now I did curvet wildly! I couldn't get the bow headed toward the island; the wind spun me back every time. I was amazed at the canoe, usually so obedient to Lee's slightest gesture; it was up in arms against me. With no authority at all, I went drifting down the lake to an unknown destination.

I began to have misgivings. What *was* going to happen to me? It looked as if I might blow across the lake.

If I did that, I'd have to wait on the far shore till the wind went down. Probably I'd be there all night. I had no matches with me for a fire — not even a coat for a cover. And Lee would be frightened about me. For that matter I'd be horribly frightened about myself. In the mornings we always found footprints of things that had walked along the shores in the night. I didn't want to stay on a dark shore and meet them. But I'd never dare go back into the forest depths —

I looked despairingly back at Lee, safe on our cliff.

He was just giving me up as hopeless. Resignedly, as I watched, he sat down and began to unlace his boots.

The next thing I knew he was swimming to the mainland, and then he came dashing along the rocks, parallel to my course. But I was in the lee of the island now, and sheltered from the wind; so by peculiar paddling I managed to approach the shore. Lee waded out and boarded the craft, and I was ignominiously wafted homeward.

I began to wish I hadn't laughed so unrestrainedly at Lee in the afternoon. It had set a bad example.

"No sense in this, my dear! No sense in this! — And if it hadn't been for that spot of calm I suppose I'd be galloping for miles around all those deep bays, to keep you from going down the rapids at the end of the lake!"

But in spite of his hilarity I found myself hoping that he would *not* break his strong right arm, or even his left one. In fact I hoped fervently that nothing at all would happen to him. For it was evident that if anything did, it would take me years to get us back to Winton.

I awoke in the middle of the night to feel deeply thankful that I was safe on our island and not stranded on some solitary shore. I got up and slipped out of the tent to see what midnight was really like. Under an ink-black pine, looking out over the dim water, I felt strange and small.

76

The wind had died. The stillness had an inexplicable poignancy. Those immensities of land and water — they belonged to porcupines walking in the moonlight, to slender deer, and heavy shuffling bears.

I tried to picture this region in midwinter. The flawless white. Snowy hills, snowy pines with glints of hidden jade, vast levels of snowy lake. A drifted purity broken only by track patterns, from the tiny footprints of the wood mice to the great crashes of the moose. The frosted vapor coming up from the rapids, encrusting the branches with silver, drifting down the shores like the ghosts of the caribou that used to wander here. Deer standing on their hind legs to eat the cedars, a pileated woodpecker shocking the snowy silence with his scarlet and white and black. Timber wolves trotting along the ice, skirting the shores —

And at that I heard a wolf howl, far down the lake. Again the howl came, unmistakable. After the blood-curdling moose call, this seemed only pleasantly eerie, especially as it was a distant sound. Still, I went inside the tent again.

This afternoon we went over to the lily pond to read *The King's Henchman*. White water lilies lay on the black water; white birches, delicate poplars, and dark cedars were mingled on three sides. On the fourth was a gigantic hill, with straight Norway pines towering up magnificently between moss-deep rocks. Their strength was a powerful contrast to all the lacelike beauty near by.

We climbed into the branches of a pine which hung far out over the water, and dangled our feet and read Millay to our hearts' content. Then we swam in the ebony pool — so different from our usual sunny beaches — and tried picking water lilies under water.

Tomorrow we start retracing our path, so I suppose my notebook will end here. I've just noticed that I never seem to write down the last few days in any of our journeys. Probably because when my thoughts begin to turn with joy toward home, I don't want to realize the fact of departure. Probably, too, I am not as deep in the moment's adventure. Not that there is less enjoyment in these hours, but we are already changing from the present to the future tense. And then I never like to say good-by.

Lee is hurrying now to finish his sketch of the deep forest, before the light fails. It is his last chance, for we are starting out at dawn tomorrow morning.

It is time for us to go. The food pack is very light to lift. There is a look of autumn in the sunlight now, though no frosty air has touched us. The blueberry leaves have been crimson ever since we've been here, but now the stray birches are shining yellow among the dark pines down the shore.

Yet we do not need to hurry too fast on our way back, for we have five days left before we must reach Winton. We mean to take practically the same paths and portages. The leaves along the stony hills will be flaming gold and scarlet soon — we are looking forward to that.

But I don't want to leave. I'll always remember this place and long for it a little. Islands of gold and green, the wind in great branches, an owl's call in the rainy dusk, the scent of our wood smoke drifting across the moonlight. It will be like a lost kingdom.

ACKNOWLEDGMENTS

In so informal and personal a book as this, a conventional preface in the usual place might have come between the reader and the good companions who were sharing their experience with him. But now that the journey is ended, and the spell broken, we can thank those who made it possible.

First, of course, Mrs. Jaques, who graciously consented to expand into a book sketches contributed to the *American Girl* and to the *Portal*. To the discerning editors of these magazines we make grateful acknowledgment of the permission to reprint those parts of the book which appeared in their pages.

And equally Mr. Jaques, for complementing his wife's sensitivity and gaiety with his knowledge of the wilderness and with the sure vigor and beauty of his drawing. Mr. Jaques' bird habitat groups in the American Museum of Natural History are the delight of thousands. His paintings illustrate *Florida Bird Life, The Birds of Minnesota*, and *Oceanic Birds of South America;* he has done black and white sketches for many of the books by Dr. Frank M. Chapman. Some of the drawings in this book are adapted from illustrations for an article in *Natural History*. We thank its editors for permission to use them in this way.

The Publishers

SNOWSHOE
COUNTRY

by FLORENCE PAGE JAQUES

illustrations by FRANCIS LEE JAQUES

To Dick, Dorothy, Bill, Lynette, and Jerry

Here is no account of struggle and hardship; rather, it is the story of a release from the tenseness of present-day life. Its aim is a simple one—to give a picture of what anyone might find, through the winter, in the border country of Minnesota and Canada. Through this wilderness of lakes and forests my husband and I, when we were first married, took the canoe trip we pictured in *Canoe Country*; here is the same land in another guise.

The Rainy Lake watershed is a wide network of over fifteen thousand lakes, including the Superior National Forest of more than three million acres and the Quetico Provincial Park in Canada, which is larger still. We first went, for the early autumn, to Basswood Lake in the center of this region; for the winter experiences we were near its eastern boundary, on Gunflint Lake, and at the last we had a few delightful days on Rainy Lake in the western area. Because of lack of space and in the interest of unity I have transferred a few incidents—the Saganaga day of driving was really on Rainy Lake, as was the grave of the little Indian boy who fell from a cliff, and the bear was met in North Bay on Basswood.

For advice on the region, for generous hospitality, and for valuable suggestions on this book we owe a debt of gratitude to many Minnesota people. Our thanks are especially due to Ernest C. Oberholtzer, Frank B. Hubachek, Thomas S. Roberts, Frederick Highland, Joseph Kerntz, Justine and William Kerfoot, Bruce Kerfoot, Dudy Thomas, Gustav Swanson, Grace Lee Nute, Sigurd and Elizabeth Olson, John and Elvin

Hendrickson, Robert Watts, Marie Aftreith, Harriet Rust, Clare Hendee, Henry Jacobs, Shaler Aldous, Don and Leyna Wilson, and Ahbutch, or Lillian Plummer.

And finally we wish to express our deep gratitude and appreciation to the University of Minnesota for the fellowship, given through their Regional Writing Program, which made this experience possible, and especially to Margaret S. Harding of the University of Minnesota Press, who conceived the idea of these companion books.

F. P. J.

July 1944

LIST OF ILLUSTRATIONS

Snowshoe Country

Basswood Lake, October 12th

We awoke to our first snowstorm. The cadence of the white flakes falling through these immense pines was like that of attacking battalions, with our small lodge a blockhouse held against them. We had pancakes for breakfast to fortify ourselves.

Then we dashed out hilariously into the storm. All the forest was white with dim green undertones; the horizontal branches of our great pines held ledges of snow precariously against the misted sky. In the marsh the tamaracks had not yet lost their needles and their lemon yellow—a strange, clear color—was only faintly veiled, so that they looked as if moonlight were entangled in their branches.

Through the muskeg and the spruce thickets the deer tracks were patterned, the scarlet leaf-stars of the bunchberry shone above the snow, and chickadees, upside down rather more than usual, were calling in great glee. We could see snowflakes float down from incredible heights against the blurred pine tops. The storm, so gay and spirited, made me want to laugh aloud; this first meeting with winter is a very happy one.

We could not bear to lose one moment of it. I wanted to try the snowshoes hanging on the walls, but Lee laughed at the idea of putting them on for a few inches of snow. Instead we went out on the water, the first time I ever drifted through a snowstorm in a canoe. The ducks swimming among the bulrushes and yellow lily pads flew off across the lake, and a deer at the edge of the grass made long leaps into the white forest. The storm hid the distant shores—only the nearest islands floated, suspended in snowflakes.

3

Around the point the north wind hit us and we paddled along in two storms, one of white flakes and one of gold aspen leaves. Then we heard geese crying from a great distance. They came, flock after flock, flying in long V's over the snowy spruces, dimly seen. But their calls were as clear as bugle notes. No music gives the challenging triumph of those cries.

Tonight a dazzling moonrise lured us out again. All the lake and hills were snowlit and the silver scrolls of clouds that tumbled along the horizon were repeated exactly in the bright water. The whole world was white except for the orange moonpath. There was even light in the shadows. Under the pines our little house, with its yellow windows and the smoke drifting in a soft banner, looked snug and secure.

October 14th

The snow has vanished and the birch and aspen stand bare on the shores, which before the storm were solid masses of yellow and orange, like marigolds in the sun. The wanigan on which the lumber crew have been living, and a smaller houseboat, pulled by the launch, came back to camp this afternoon. A horse walked sedately out of the wanigan (though I don't believe the statement that he slept in an upper bunk coming over). Now we eat in the cookhouse with the lumberjacks. They have a wonderful cook ("we eat yust like millionaires, only more," as Eli says), but no one talks at meals. "Eat and run" is the literal fact.

I laugh when I remember the doubt I felt about this place when we were approaching it! Not about the lodge that Fred Highland had so generously lent us, for everyone told us it was a charming place. But as all the lumber camps I'd seen had been unsightly, littered spots, I was unprepared for the perfection of neatness at "Hi's Place." These small and sturdy buildings of yellow logs standing beneath pine shadows, with clean brown needles and bright partridge berries covering the ground between them—how far from my idea of a lumber camp! Most thrilling of all were the tiny pines planted everywhere through the forest.

Our host had written us: "We plant young pines wherever we can, for future forests, and just now we're salvaging cut timber which would otherwise lie wasted. We're also interested in salvaging Finns—those who can't get jobs because of age or drink or misfortune." We were tremen-

4

1. RANGER STATION. 2. RANGER'S CABIN NO. 16. 3. HOIST BAY. 4. BACK BAY. 5. WIND BAY. 6. FROG BAY. 7. NORTH BAY. 8. MERRIAM BAY. 9. NORWAY POINT. 10. U. S. POINT. 11. CANADIAN POINT. 12. UPPER BASSWOOD FALLS. 13. LOWER BASSWOOD FALLS. 14. CROOKED LAKE. 15. MOOSE BAY. 16. ROBINSON LAKE. 17. FOUR MILE PORTAGE.

dously interested in this conservation experiment. But I had felt a little shy at joining such an array of Finnish loggers!

However, when we arrived, the crew was at work on the Canadian shores; only two were here. And we have enjoyed Eli and Otto immensely. Eli is a gnomelike figure in a green plaid shirt, stagged orange trousers, stubby boots, and unruly hair—rather like a hilarious Thurber drawing. The fact that he has only every other tooth rather adds to the gaiety of his grin. He acted as a guide last summer, and one day he took two dowagers fishing. One of them said nervously, "Isn't this boat awfully tippy?" "Boat never be tippy," said Eli reassuringly, "you too goddam fat."

Eli is usually good-natured, but he lost his temper one day. "Damn sonofabitch," he stormed. "Joe, how you say sonofabitch in English?"

Otto is more like a chunky wood carving, solid and square. At first I thought he looked melancholy, but that was only because he was reluctant to speak English. Now he is very gay and he looks after us beautifully, bringing us home-baked bread and rolls and doughnuts, showing us the terrifying bear trap he has concocted, and explaining the sauna, the Finnish bathhouse. (Unluckily, I didn't understand his explanations completely and almost blew myself sky-high in a steam explosion by pouring dippers of water, instead of a scant half dipper, on the hot stones.)

When Joe Kerntz, who is Hi's partner, took us over to see where the men were working in Canada, we met another interesting Finnish logger, an older man, Matti Seikkla. It was he who built our beautifully proportioned lodge from Hi's verbal instructions and a sketch made in the snow with a twig. Legends of his prodigious strength have been told up and down this timber country for years; in his young days in the mines he carried with ease a pneumatic hammer weighing more than seven hundred pounds. Among all the older Finnish men his pronouncements are law today.

On this point the men are salvaging the huge trees that were torn up by the roots and knocked over by bulldozers in the lumbering done by a Canadian company last year. It looks as if war had devastated this place, as indeed it has, for it is the great need for lumber that causes this desolation. But we were amazed at the great amounts of timber saved by this crew. The logs were floated in rafts along the shore, held by boom logs chained end to end.

In the early days loggers could come to this region only by water, and trees were cut only along lakes and rivers. Then the railroads reached larger areas, and now the most remote places are accessible by air. One hundred and fifty lumberjacks were brought in here by airplane last spring.

But Joe says that next spring he will have hundreds of little pines flown in and planted here, so I must credit the airplane with aid in saving forests as well as destroying them. And of course the air patrol, the "eyes of the rangers," has saved millions of acres from fires.

The men here were living in the wanigan, which is a big houseboat with a double tier of bunks. In its kitchen we had coffee and doughnuts. Then Joe took us in the launch to the post of two Canadian rangers, the

Hendricksons, where we had coffee again, and bread and cheese, in a cheerful kitchen. We had music too, for both the brothers (Swedish, though the younger has the dash and mischief of a French Canadian) play violins. It was very pleasant to sit and drink coffee and listen to their melodies while the rain patted gently on the roof.

This afternoon was almost like summer again, and we went in the canoe to Back Bay, which is wide and shallow, with many islands. High water ruined the wild rice this year; there was only a scattering of pale stems. But slim bulrushes made delightful arches, and lily pads of all shapes and sizes lay about us. Large yellow ones, heart-shaped leaves of green with rosy underfacings, small oval ones in crimson and orange, and delicately pointed ones of olive green. I can't decide whether I like them better when the blue sky reflects between their patterns so that they are inlaid on turquoise, or when the water, dark and clear, reveals their bronze stems curving down to the rippled, sun-shot sand.

Mergansers ran before us on the water, and warblers ran around on the lily pads as if they thought they were waterfowl. Paddling around a rocky ledge with twisted pines, suddenly we were startled by a terrifying commotion. Just above us an eagle leaped from a low branch and flapped away. We had caught him napping, and he thought we were nightmares in person. It is really very gratifying to frighten an eagle.

October 15th

Hi and his duck shooters arrive tomorrow. They are to live on the wanigan while the crew move into the bunkhouse. Hi will not hear of our giving up this lodge.

Our surroundings have the noblest beauty. Hi bought the land to make sure that this glorious forest, with many pines more than two hundred years old, would never be cut. Beneath their massive blue-green boughs the lodge stands, low and spacious, built with meticulous skill of aspen logs scraped and waxed till the interior is like muted sunlight. From the wide windows we looked out, the first evening, through pine branches to green-gold, rippled water, and I shall always think of green ripples and gold sun when I remember this forest lodge.

The living room has a massive granite fireplace, and over it a great pane of glass is laid into the sloping roof, so that we look up from the

fire to see pine tops and clouds and sky above us. When the moon shines through the low windows we have firelight, starlight, moonlight, all at once!

We have used the lodge as headquarters for our canoeing trips. How glorious it has been to be back in this border wilderness! For canoeing there is no place like it in the world, and there is no country we have loved more deeply.

This fall we have had, not one, but three canoe trips! Our first, in the extreme end of North Bay, was a stormy one; we even had a hailstorm battering at our tent. But it was exciting to camp in such weather, and as we were in a medley of channels and islands we were not completely windbound. The wild squalls only enhanced the escarpments of rosy granite, hung with cedar and pine and softened by puffs of gray moss, and the fleets of islands in the waterways. Beavers, working with acute industry to get large piles of willow and aspen stored beneath the water before winter overtook them, were our constant companions. Warblers flitting through the small waterfalls along the dams, in among the spray and wet green leaves, gave diminutive ballets for us. An insufferable chipmunk took over my camp kitchen and was in and out of the packsacks until I forgot that one should never fight with anyone smaller than oneself, and at night the woodmice, in a spirit of adventure, scaled our tent as if it were a Matterhorn. The whole first night here I stayed wide awake, as one always does the first night of camping—excess of happiness, probably.

Our next trip was like a midsummer one, so balmy that only the countless yellow aspens glittering against blue air and reflecting in the water like nets of gold sequins could make us believe it was October. In Merriam Bay we camped in great stands of Norway pine, for "we'll never have another chance to camp in such deep forest," Lee said. Our tent looked very tiny under these columned pines, among huge, lichened boulders and billows of emerald moss. Here was the strange half-light—a luminous, liquid, golden aura—which we had found before in forests of Norway pine.

And our last trip was the greatest delight of all, for we went with Elvin Hendrickson, the ranger, over part of the route we had taken long ago on our first canoeing. We saw again the Basswood Falls and the Picture Rocks; our three circle lakes looked even lovelier as scores of black ducks flew up against deep-orange grass and coppery branches.

We drifted along our dream river with the still reeds and white boulders until a log dam made us portage. Here we stopped so that Lee could make a drawing of the dam, which had a sluiceway through which the logs had floated. The pressure of the water had buckled it and it had been propped with logs and rocks, and still we wondered how it held.

On Robinson Lake we found a deserted lumber camp built of upright logs. Forlorn and picturesque, it stood between cliffs in a little valley. In the big cookhouse we cooked on an old stove that barely held together, and we slept on the floor.

We lay in the dark with mice ranging far and near, and Elvin told stories of snarling wolves and bear, of moose charging camps, and of ferocious wolverines. The next morning I said, "Elvin, where are all those fierce animals you told us about? I haven't seen anything larger than a mouse!"

"Well, I tell you. This is too wild country for them. The game is scared of this wild place."

I will remember every moment of these camping trips.

But in our lodge we find an equal contentment. Every evening we go out on the water at sunset or into the twilight forest. Last night we paddled to a lake rimmed by a vast circle of bright gold hills—like a blue bubble banded by sparkling crystals, with foamy clouds afloat in it and our canoe only a tiny speck in its center. Then a loon cried. As Thoreau says: "He muttered a long-drawn unearthly howl, probably more like that of a wolf than any bird; as when a beast puts his muzzle to the ground and deliberately howls!" Any melody here, the whitethroat's song, for instance, would have had an oversweetness, but this sound added a savage touch that gave the evening a sharp edge of splendor.

Tonight, as we walked back through the lofty pines, there were deer all about, though they were so wild that we saw only white flashes as they vanished.

Then we became involved in a muskeg swamp. I am fond of walking on muskeg, but not in the twilight. We had to leap from hummock to hummock, and I was afraid of leaping lightly at a bear. There were black stumps about, any one of which might have had fur. Lee gets me into the beariest places, I thought rebelliously; if I do hit a bear, it will serve him right—*he'll* be sorry!

As we made firm ground we saw, under the pines ahead of us, a beautiful deer, a buck, with four-point horns! We moved forward, closer and closer—we came within ten yards. The buck must have thought we were twilight shadows. For a long time we played a game of tag in slow motion around the dusky hill. He wasn't at all afraid, and once we got within five paces of him. Lee thought it would be quite a triumph to drive him back to our lodge, but at last he slipped away and we let him go.

This was a strange incident, for all the deer we've seen have been extremely wary. But Joe says that occasionally a deer seems to lose all sense of caution and will follow a man almost into camp.

October 17th

Hi and his guests arrived last night to take possession of the house-boat. They were in wild spirits at the prospect of a week's hunting, and we did not have to worry about the lack of conversation at supper. Joe blazes like a bonfire when he talks of duck shooting. I have seen ardent

13

duck hunters, but never one like Joe. Eli beams at the shouting and laughter. He is rather touching tonight, very clean and neat, like a youngster at the beginning of a party.

Most of the days of this duck season have been so warm and sunny it has not been good shooting weather, and the main flight of ducks has not yet come down. But the greatest joy in any hunting is the sense of high expectancy, the same keen excitement we felt as children on the eve of a holiday—no knowing *what* may happen! We can have that even in dreamy weather.

And I am lucky in that I have as exciting a time, or more so, on the unsuccessful days as on the successful ones. When black ducks fly up from the reeds toward the tamaracks, or bluebills come over a tawny marsh, it is their wild and joyful flight that makes my heart leap. Nothing has a sharper glory than wildfowl. They make one feel that life *could* be infinitely more vivid. They are symbols of that intensity we experience at the high moments of our existence.

October 19th

This week is a holiday one. Everyone does whatever he likes all day, and we all meet at supper to tell of our adventures.

Hi is like a Fourth of July sparkler; he glitters with energy. This vigor, however, makes us all enjoy ourselves more and not less, for he does not, like some indefatigable hosts I have known, expect his guests to keep up with his quicksilver roaming. He is up with Joe all night, bringing rafts of logs across the lake while the wind is down, dashing about all day, making plans for winter, seeing the men, and getting in a few hours of hunting and fishing besides.

Today was quite eventful. The duck hunters at Wind Bay met a man who fled into the slashings; he might have been an escaped German prisoner from Canada. Then a visitor failed to anchor his seaplane properly, and it blew into our cedar tree and broke the swimming dock. Later we met one of our partridge hunters in the woods, and as he told us of walking miles without seeing a partridge one walked calmly out in front of us. Infuriated, he picked up a rock, heaved it at the bird, and to his surprise knocked it dead. "Gosh!" he said. "Hi asked me not to shoot any within rifle range of the lodge. But then, I didn't *shoot* it!"

14

Tonight there were twenty of us for supper, crew, guests, and Big Buck Sletten, famous as a woodsman and guide and still more famous for practical jokes. He says that when he helped one year at the Trading Post a little boy noticed the hide of a spotted calf and asked what it was. "That's the skin of a fish," Buck told him. "Fish don't have fur," the boy objected. "You ain't never seen them in the winters up here, hev you?" Buck asked. He is a veritable mine of misinformation.

October 20th

Our last day, and the great flocks of ducks have not come down. Today, though it was stormy, our whole party went in the launch for partridge shooting on the Basswood Falls portage. There we had sandwiches and Joe made a blazing fire for our camp coffee. Hi quoted Stewart Edward White, "We lit a campfire and immediately it was home." That is what I have felt with all our autumn campfires.

High on the hills Lee and I found partridges. Scrambling up broken squares of granite, with the smell of autumn in the wind, we swung through billows of noisy leaves until one or more of the brown birds whirred up through the trees or down over a cliff.

When they are on the ground these ruffed grouse seem as placid as fowls, but they rise in the air with a startling rush, dodging through branches on short, powerful wings, their flight swift and reckless. I like partridge shooting better than duck shooting. I have compunctions, but not the vivid pang I feel when a duck drops. The partridge does not have the adventurous ardor, the unparalleled joy, which make wildfowl one of the wonders of the world.

We went home through such rough water that everyone was drenched in buckets of spray. Tonight was our gala dinner, for this was the first day for whitefish and Big Buck had been smoking them in the smokehouse. Freshly smoked whitefish is the best fish in the world, and the party certainly did justice to it.

The fish made everyone thirsty, and Elvin, one of the Canadian rangers, took one long cool drink and slapped himself on the chest. "That's made a new man of me," he stated. And then added hastily, "And that man needs a drink too!"

16

The last morning here. I took myself along the white pine trail, gray and misty and glamorous. For the last time I picked a spray of sweet gale, to smell its tantalizing scent, half bayberry, half lemon thyme, and pulled a little goldthread plant to see if it really did have goldthread roots. Once more I looked up into the great pines, following with my eyes the almost imperceptible curve of the strong boughs, the lovely outward sweep of feathery needles.

I treasure everything about this fall, but most of all the intimacy with these ancient trees. They are great friends in every sense of the word; they give as strong and true a comradeship as human companions ever can. Here they will stand. Whatever happens in the world, we will know they are here. To be remembered if we never come again, to welcome us if we return. Their stillness is not resigned or patient, it is full of vitality; they give *assurance* to life. "Peace I leave with you, my peace I give unto you. Let not your heart be troubled. Neither let it be afraid." That is the spirit of this place.

Duluth, October 23d

We have had five weeks of holiday canoeing. Now I go soberly and in the fear of God to live in a northern winter.

I never really meant to do this! Lee has said many times, "Let's do a book on the winter woods. Let's spend a winter in northern Minnesota!" and I always said, "Yes, let's." Without the smallest idea that we ever would.

However, I am so thankful for our autumn canoe trips that I am willing to live in a snowdrift now, if that is the price I have to pay. But I am appalled at myself. Women in the winter woods always sound so robust and stalwart!

Just the same, here we go, to enjoy (!) the winter wilderness and to get acquainted with its people. When we left Basswood Lake we went, by launch and truck and launch again, to Ely, and from there we came by train to Duluth. Tomorrow we take a bus along the north shore of Lake Superior a hundred miles or so, and from Grand Marais we start north on the Gunflint Trail. The Kerfoots at Gunflint Lake are not keeping their lodge open this winter, but they have a cabin we can

use. There we can live for several months as two of the country's "winterers"—*hivernants*, as the old fur traders said.

Gunflint Lodge, October 25th

Out on a Duluth street corner in the dark, long before dawn, we waited for the Wilderness Express. This hybrid, half bus and half truck, will be our only connection with the outside world at Gunflint Lake. It brings the mail, carries supplies, and takes us in and out.

It had rained all night, and the North Shore, with its black rocks and dusky trees painted with tips of yellow flame, looked as savage as a leopard. At Grand Marais, once a trading post of John Jacob Astor's fur company, we left Lake Superior and started north on the Gunflint Trail.

On this road, an ancient Indian trail, we plunged into forest and drove almost fifty miles, up and down roller-coaster hills and around lakes. And at last, "There's Gunflint," said the driver of the Express.

We turned off the Trail into a side road that led along a blue lake, and after crossing several hills we came to a sign, "Gunflint Lodge," held by a ferocious wooden chieftain with an upraised tomahawk, and were announced by a burst of howls from up the hill. What an ominous welcome, I thought.

When we stopped in a clearing in front of a long, low building, rather like a western ranch house, a husky chained to the porch set up a howling answer to the other dogs, and Bill Kerfoot, tall and lanky, with round glasses and surprised eyebrows, came out to meet us. His greeting was enthusiastic; little did we suspect that he had no idea what to do with us.

He took us into the lodge, and Leo, the driver, came too, in search of coffee. There was an office with a wide room on each side and a huge kitchen behind it. "There's the lounge, to the right," our host said, "but I haven't built the fire yet. The kitchen is warm; would you like to come in there?"

"May we see where we're going to live first?" I asked.

"You certainly can," Bill said. "Leo, the girls left that lemon pie for you. Help yourself!"

He led us outdoors and we took a wooded path. Several hundred yards away from the lodge a small brown cabin stood in a little clearing of its own, with spruce and cedar about it, and tall aspens swaying high above its roof.

"Here she is," said Bill.

He opened the door on a small kitchen. Then came a square living room with windows on three sides, and off that a bedroom and an enclosed porch.

The cabin looked rather like Mother Hubbard's cupboard to me. In the center of the living room stood an oil drum on legs, battered and black and slightly off center. This was the barrel stove, and Lee was looking at it with admiration. "That's the thing that will keep us warm," he said enthusiastically.

"Will you want to do your own cooking at first?" Bill asked, I thought a trifle hopefully.

"No," said Lee. "It takes time we'd rather spend outdoors. Besides, this kitchen isn't heated, is it?"

"Well, no," Bill said. "Ah, you see, Mrs. Kerfoot is in Florida with her people just now, and Aggie, the cook, has gone to the hospital for a few days, so one of the guests is doing the cooking at present."

"Oh," we said, rather nonplussed. "Can you manage?"

1. MAGNETIC LAKE. 2. LOON LAKE. 3. NORTH LAKE. 4. SOUTH LAKE. 5. HEIGHT OF LAND PORTAGE. 6. GRANITE RIVER. 7. RIB LAKE TRAIL. 8. SEAGULL LAKE. 9. NORTHERN LIGHTS LAKE.

"Sure," said Bill. "Ahbutch, the Indian girl who helps us in summer, is here, and we have three other guests. But it's all pretty casual. I hope you won't mind."

Outside, a small, active brook—I've always wanted a pet brook—leaped gaily down through rocks and cedar roots to the lake. One path led up the woods to the road, the other to the lodge.

"Let's go out on the lake and explore," Lee suggested.

Bill gave us a canoe and we started off. The country seems far wilder than Basswood. Here are the long sawtooth mountains that run up from the south in a long slope and break into abrupt cliffs. In between them lie long, narrow lakes. There are hardly any transverse valleys. When we got out on the lake, a great cliff shouldered up behind Gunflint Lodge, making it look very small.

We paddled across to the narrows leading into Magnetic Bay, a lake where deposits of iron oxide throw compasses into a frenzy, to the confusion of newcomers. Back along the north shore of Gunflint, under

22

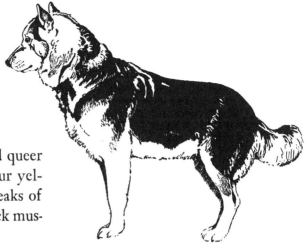

low-growing cedar, we found queer rocks of rust color and sulphur yellow. These rocks contain streaks of the flint used in the old flintlock muskets by the *voyageurs*.

We returned to the lodge just as the animals were being fed. Whittles is the dog by the porch, a black and cream beauty with topaz eyes and sharp, upstanding ears. There are two fuzzy puppies at the back door, with their tawny mother Ginger. The other sled dogs, up the hill, chained to their kennels, made such a furious uproar when they saw the food buckets, leaping in the air like tethered demons, that I'm not sure whether there are six or a dozen. Then there is Ferdinand, a bull calf, bought because the Kerfoots couldn't decide whether to get a sheep or a goat to crop the grass, and a bulky white pig.

We asked Bill if any of the sled dogs were dangerous. "No," he said. "Of course we had to look out for that, with strangers around all summer. A full-blooded husky or Malamute may be treacherous. When the wolf strain predominates they can't be trusted. So we crossed a husky with a Norwegian elkhound, and that gives us a type which is absolutely dependable and yet has the strength and endurance necessary for a sled dog."

Inside the lodge supper was ready in the big kitchen. Here was the guest from Arizona who was acting as chef—dark haired, dark eyed, and throwing off energy like a small geyser. And Ahbutch, an attractive Chippewa girl, who to my horror was nicknamed Butchie—such a gentle, aristocratic person couldn't have a more incongruous name! A fervent fisherman and a young lawyer, here by his doctor's orders, completed the party. Oh no, there was an enormous black cat with white whiskers and eyebrows like George Bernard Shaw's.

"We saw a cabin on Magnetic," we said to Bill. "Does anyone live there?"

"Yes, Butchie's people," he answered. "And her aunt and cousin live on this lake. Then the Ambroses—he's a guide and a trapper—live across the narrows, and an old caretaker is two miles down the shore. These are our neighbors, and good ones. Of course, good neighbors are more important here than in most places; in winter it can even be a question of survival."

After dinner we had a fire in the lounge, and Arizona sang for us. I've always heard of these fabulous daughters of the West; Arizona is a perfect specimen, and I'm as thrilled to know her as I would be to find a heath hen or a great auk.

She is certainly a most festive person. Warmhearted and generous, never out of temper, she makes everyone have a good time whether they want to or not. Nothing stops her. She likes to conquer a situation, no matter what the difficulties. Now she has seen this region (and knows more about it in a month than many people would find out in a lifetime), but she is staying on to help Bill and Butchie out of a tight spot. "You'd all leave if there was no one to manage the kitchen," she says, "and we help neighbors out, in *my* country!"

She treats Butchie as she would a younger sister, bullying her, confiding in her, helping her to make the most of herself. Just now she is determined that Butchie shall learn to read and write, but she is lighthearted in her zeal and Butchie laughs with her, without self-consciousness.

Last night we listened to her varied repertoire of songs. Her singing is unique, a combination of baby talk and torch singing which reduces us to helpless laughter. (Except Butchie, who is too loyal to laugh.) To see Arizona sing *You Great Big Beautiful Doll* as she looks up at each man in turn with adoring brown eyes is something to remember.

October 25th

Starting out early this morning, we went down the Granite River, the lovely canoe route to Saganaga Lake.

There is *nothing* like journeying in a canoe! Traveling any other way, we are separate from our environment, but a canoe is a bit of nature, like a stray leaf; it is too frail to be a barrier. This morning the blue water and white rapids, the huge cloud bubbles, and the strong scent of the pines produced in me that almost unbearable ecstasy that I had found before in our canoe country.

I had no idea how intense the sense of escape from the hourly shocks of wartime New York would be. I knew this wilderness was sure to release me in some measure, but not how great the weight it could lift from me. This sense of utter freedom and delight is what we must hold for our youngsters who come back from fighting, I said to myself; this wild liberty *must* be kept inviolate for them.

At lunchtime we stopped on the rocks, where a huge cedar twisted and bent above us. Warblers were lingering here, flickering in the treetops, taking small trial flights and coming back again, like little practice runs on a harpsichord.

"How wonderful," I cried, "to be where it's as unspoiled as it was three hundred years—" and then I stumbled over a tin can. "Damn people!" I said.

There were other tin cans, torn maps, and old sneakers. How anyone who loves the outdoors enough to come to these faraway places can ruin them for others I can't understand. But I wish I were Circe! What joy I would take in changing these beasts into pigs, into warthogs, and driving them into the wallows where they belong!

While we ate lunch two golden eagles came circling far above us, passing each other and turning sidewise in their frolic, soaring up on an air current and tumbling down again. Then we heard the queerest hubbub up the hill, and climbed the rocks to investigate it.

Under a thick spruce two porcupines faced each other, nose to nose, snarling and growling. I thought they were sworn enemies, but when at last they turned aside one kept on with small reproachful murmurs, long after the quarrel was over. Evidently it was a domestic squabble. And then, up in a cedar, we saw a third porcupine, small but very self-assured, gathering cedar to its breast till it looked like a large bouquet. Here was the *femme fatale!*

We started out again in the canoe, and as we skirted along a granite shore a belated bear came ambling out and stood blackly silhouetted against the sky, looking across the water. As we came closer, he turned to look us over, arrogant and unalarmed. Then he sniffed in a disparaging manner and vanished before we could retaliate.

Bears have been unusually prevalent this year. We had one on our back porch at Basswood and another broke into a nearby lodge, smashing the icebox and many dishes. They have even invaded small towns. Blueberries have been scarce and the bears are hungry.

But I know now what to do when I meet one. For at Basswood I read the *Kalevala*, the Finnish national epic, very ancient, most charming in its minute descriptions of nature (and if I hadn't met Eli and Otto I would never have read it); and now I know the charm, the "wizard saying" for getting rid of a bear.

Thou, O Otso, forest-apple,
Woodland bear, with honeyed fingers . . .
Wander like the golden cuckoo,
Like the dove of silver brightness,
Like a little fish in ocean;
Hide thy claws within thy hair-foot,
Shut thy wicked teeth in darkness . . .
Throw thy malice to the mountains,
And thy hunger to the pine trees,
Sink thy teeth within the aspens!

As we came home in the green afterglow, which in this northern land has a clarity that stops the breath, the water and the air were still, and the shores stood solid with rich plum and topaz and strong green. As the afterglow paled the shores grew more massive, with a complete emptiness above and below them—an emptiness in which two crescent moons, one high and one low, floated.

A loon was crying weirdly, and its echo, coming back, made it wail louder still. The Indians say the loon cries, "Oh, where are you? where are you?" when it wails in this way.

Out in the wide lake we found emptiness still more vast—the canoe seemed about to fall or rise into infinite space. It was a relief to take up the paddle and plunge it into something as tangible as water. As the shores grew blacker, the moon in the sky grew brighter, the one in the lake more nebulous, and a flight of ducks went over us, calling through the night.

October 27th

Here we are in a real birch forest. I've been in a birch *wood* before, but never in a great birch forest where thousands of the trees make lovely repetitions of "black branches up a snow-white trunk," far into the distance.

We have been gathering birch bark for winter stationery and for kindling our fire. Now Lee is drawing the stumps and roots of cedars, while I am comfortably curled up on a canoe cushion against a log. It's snowing very lazily on this mild afternoon. White snow wandering through white birches from a white sky.

The flakes are almost like spring petals falling. This afternoon has a feeling of *promise* about it, such as April gives us, but it is a far more mysterious promise than that of spring.

Our canoe lies below us on the rocky shore. We have been out in it every day, exploring Gunflint Lake. No matter how promising the morning as we start out now we are sure to have to fight black swells and plunging whitecaps coming home. When we came across the bay today a squall suddenly hit us, spinning us completely around, although we purposely sat low in the canoe. We had no more weight than an acorn cup. It made me realize how fortunate we have been not to encounter a real gale at any time.

The snowflakes are falling faster on my notebook now, and Lee is hurrying to finish his drawing. No more lazy balmy days for me, he says; no more canoeing. Winter has come.

October 29th

The Wilderness Express came late yesterday afternoon. From now on it will bring mail only once a week, on Saturdays! Everyone came in and had coffee in the kitchen—Benny Ambrose, the guide from across the lake, who tells us entertaining stories; two Indians, a mother and her daughter Tempest, with more than a ton of provisions which they will portage far up Saganaga; and Charlie Olsen, the Norwegian caretaker who lives by himself down the shore. He is eighty-two, small, with mild blue eyes and a fiery manner.

Arizona insists on giving us wonderful four-course dinners, in spite of our protests. She loves to amaze us. After dinner we all play Chinese checkers to see who will do the dishes; it is extraordinary how exciting Chinese checkers can be under such circumstances. It transpires gradually that Aggie has had blood poisoning and her finger must be amputated. She won't be back for a long time.

We played cards all evening. Bill manages his variously tempered guests very adroitly. He was headed for the diplomatic service when he met the north woods and Justine, and his talents aren't wasted as a resort host. He keeps us all amused at one another. His insouciance carries him along easily. Though he seems to wander leisurely about, things get done; just in time, occasionally, but not too late.

When we left the lodge to go home we were stopped short by the strange colors of the Northern Lights. Down on the dock we stood spellbound. Lee has seen them many times, but never such an astounding display. Weird yellow spirals shot into the sky through whirlpools of twisting pink and orange and dark purple. Great shimmers of pallor shook from horizon to zenith, and searchlight rays streamed up and then bent like broken grass stems. It was unearthly—it seemed just that. It had nothing to do with natural life; it came from another plane of existence. I had heard this was true, but I was not prepared for the uncanny reality, when, above a flat arc of lurid red, dim and gigantic figures marched in rapid flight across the north. There they were, there *something* was, hastening to the unknown.

November 1st

Snowing today. We decided to get ready for cold weather, and moved into the living room of our cabin. The unheated bedroom will make a fine closet, the kitchen is already the woodshed. These rooms and the enclosed porch will act as storm windows, Lee said, and keep this room comfortable.

On the big table I've spread the scarlet pareu Lee brought me from his South Seas expedition. Haitian bandanas cover the smaller ones. Sketches and maps pinned on the walls and vines and pine boughs make our little house seem gay and very cheerful. The kerosene lamps shine brightly, and I have at last ceased to expect an explosion whenever I turn one low.

Last night Butchie's brother George, a handsome Chippewa guide and trapper, came over with Bobby, their thirteen-year-old nephew. Bobby had never been to a Hallowe'en party, so we had one for him, with oranges for jack o' lanterns and apple bobbing and games. We enjoyed it and so did the Indians. Butchie says she has never had such a holiday time. And since it has rained all day without a stop and there was nothing we could do outdoors, we decided to have a ship's concert and captain's dinner tonight. Bobby was to go home this noon, but he was agog at a second party and stayed eagerly in the background all day.

We all dressed for dinner, the rule being to look as brilliant as possible—most of us wore red. In the midst of our frivolity we heard a truck coming through the downpour, and though we threatened to leave Bill alone in his gala finery, we were merciful and stood by. The visitors were Finns from the sawmill near Loon Lake. They looked a little startled, but they joined the party without much reluctance. Finns sing far louder than Indians do!

November 2d

Tonight we had whitefish and trout, sent over by Butchie's mother. Nettahwense is a full-blooded Chippewa. ("Ojibway" is the more formal term, but the people here say "Chippewa.") She speaks no English and clings to the ancient Indian religion, as they say many border Indians do, though most tribes, even near the Arctic Circle, have taken over the white man's beliefs.

We had guests again tonight. The first snow has evidently made people remember that they will soon be winterbound, and they are visiting while they can, roaming up and down the Trail. Val Ambrose, a graduate of Ohio State, B.A. and M.A., who is married to the trapper across the lake, came in with a guest, and a couple from Loon Lake came over. Then two Indians appeared. Arizona has made our kitchen into a night club; we have moved the piano in there, and she cooks with one hand and plays accompaniments to her songs with the other, ruffling the Finns' hair and chucking the Indians under the chin as she flits. She conquers the enormous, ancient kitchen range as she would a refractory bronco.

To our amazement she mentioned tonight that she is a grandmother. No one was ever less like a grandmother than Arizona. All we can say is that the baby, like the one in the story, must be a *very* little one.

November 5th

This has been a strange week. A lost time, between fall and winter.

We have been exploring on foot, since we no longer go canoeing. The woods are silent now. The loons have gone, the chipmunks are asleep. No sounds are heard from the chickadees or partridge or deer. The whole world seems voiceless, waiting for the snow.

We climb the high cliff, walk along the Gunflint Trail, or go east to a stand of white pines. This road ends three miles down the shore, but there is a rutted track that leads to the small sawmill near Loon Lake. Sloppy Savage, one of the Indians, has just torn down his cabin here, and his stove stands in solemn dignity on a stump by the roadside.

If we go east we always stop at Charlie Olsen's, for his small cabin is a cheerful place, with a feeding shelf for chickadees and nuthatches which is almost as big as the house itself. Charlie told us about lying in bed and seeing a bear rise up on his hind legs just outside the wide window. "I yust reach for my gun and shoot him quiet from my pillow. Don't hurt him much."

Charlie likes the small birds best, but woodpeckers are most common here. The hairy and downy woodpeckers are just alike, black and white with a red spot on the male's head, but one is half size—I never could remember which. Now I know, because a small bird is Downy. Downy has a small bill too, not a big beak like Hairy.

When I was looking them up in *The Birds of Minnesota* I found the most amazing diagram showing the hairy's tongue. Birds do get themselves up in the most peculiar fashion! The tip of a woodpecker's tongue, with few exceptions, is a rigid spearhead; the stem divides into flexible bony filaments, and they continue over the back of the skull under the skin. In the hairy they continue still farther, and the extra length curls around the right eyeball! When the bird wants to capture a grub that is snugly inside a tree, he drills a hole, then thrusts forth his tongue. The tongue unwinds and the spearhead shoots out an astonishing length to stab his victim!

More rarely do we see the Arctic three-toed and American three-toed woodpeckers. They too are black and white, but they flaunt yellow patches on their heads. The Arctic is slightly the larger and has a solid black back; the back of the American is barred. The Arctic has tremendous power in his hammering for such a small bird; his head blurs with its swift motion.

On a twilight walk last night I heard a sound that made my pulse quicken even before I realized what it was. Lee nodded at my excited look. "Geese," he said.

They were coming across the lake from the north. Louder and louder came their strong calls. Suddenly, over the fretted aspens, line after line came swiftly, the cries making the still gray air vibrate with their ineffable longing. And these were *wavering* lines! We were seeing our beloved blue geese.

I had never dreamed of seeing them this fall. On their migration from the Arctic they usually fly too high to be seen, and it was late for the flight of the beautiful winged thousands! There is no sight in the world we would rather see, and we went home in exultation.

November 7th

Lee and I climbed the high cliff back of the lodge this morning in the face of a snarling, stormy wind—a "wolf day," I called this one. On the cliff top the spruces bent from the wind and ravens whirled around us. Swaggering clouds flung past, almost low enough to engulf us.

Now I've been out to get a pail of water from our brook, lingering to watch the chickadees twirling in the bare twigs. I try to remember what the bride-adviser says in the *Kalevala*.

> *Hasten homeward like the zephyrs,*
> *Hasten like the air of autumn;*
> *Do not tarry near the streamlet,*
> *At the waters do not linger.*

But it is very difficult not to be tempted to follow the gypsy brook through the cedars and balsams.

It has begun to snow in earnest now. The lake is afroth under the wind, and the shores are gone; it is all a whirl of snow driven horizontally off the lake.

November 8th

We have a real blizzard! Twelve inches deep, and still coming down. The gale makes the lake into a stormy sea; what must Lake Superior be like? What about the freighters?

32

The drifts pile high in front of the lodge, the trees are loaded heavier and heavier. Ferdinand moans in the snow and eats icicles. The pups are aghast. But the cat goes out hunting with his accustomed nonchalance and finds mice in the middle of the storm.

When we walked to the cedar swamp this afternoon we took deep, unexpected plunges into drifts. This heavy snow is almost impossible for me to walk in. My muscles are not trained to lift heavy boots knee-high at every step. (We wear our snow boots, or rubber pacs, with feet of heavy rubber and leather halfway to the knee. Mine are far too large and the most unwieldy things I ever tried to manage.)

Though along the shore the wind was riotous, it had not touched the swamp, and there the snow stood inches high on every tilted twig, which made a strange landscape, all in white parallel planes. Lee was interested in the upward light, which illumines the place with the same diffused glow the golden leaves gave last month, though now the light has a blanched luster. The brook was ink black between the molded whiteness, and the smell of our wood smoke welcomed us as we came home down the blown and drifted trail.

Night

Blizzard after blizzard. Butchie's gentle heart was so touched by Ferdinand's groans that she has put a sweater on him, even though he has been eating the laundry from the line. (Bill swears that she even takes the chipmunks he traps in her canoe and releases them across the lake.) Now the dogs are too submerged to bark. Ginger is ruffled with snow. The wind came straight through the kitchen windows till we fastened them tight with strips. Bill has put up a second stove to keep the kitchen warm.

We are now isolated from the rest of the world. It is a queer feeling to know we can't escape and no one can reach us. In my whole life I've never been *held* to a spot like this. Bill says it's worse here tonight than it was in the famous blizzard three years ago, when so many people lost their lives.

Bill is mending his snowshoes tonight. Skis are seldom used in this forested country; snowshoes are a necessity.

November 9th

The storm has vanished, the wind has died, the lake is calm. It is the time of snow. It is strange to realize that it will now stay like this until late spring—a never-changing white landscape.

Lee climbed the cliff today, and after I swept out the cabin I walked as far as the swamp. This snow is the loveliest I have ever seen. Such stainless white—no single speck of soot or grime. This strange substance, this tangible freshness—how incredible it would seem if we did not know it was snow, with its impervious, massive appearance and its evanescent texture!

It is now so deep that I lift my feet like a circus horse. Once I entered the woods, however, I might have been floating for all I knew. I felt be-witched (white magic, not black). Bushes held triangles in their slim branches, big extravagant triangles of every kind, as if a whole migration flight of triangles had alighted there.

On into the spruces, I forgot myself and time and space. Everywhere fantastic boughs made it seem an Arctic jungle that rivaled a tropic one. Small trees were like a giant's carvings. The tall spruces had a more ab-stract character, but every bright curve had the perfection that is almost a shock. The only sounds were a faraway wind on the cliff or the swish when the snow slipped from a pine branch.

November 10th

Still snowbound. The kitchen is our clubhouse, and we are now play-ing multiple solitaire at all hours. Ahbutch is wonderful at cards. She does not make the noise that the rest of us do, but her black eyes glow and she gets quite breathless in a quiet way. We are all game addicts except Lee, who endures games as he does bad weather.

So far the single telephone wire that sags along the trail has not broken and Bill has had a wire from Justine saying that she will be home Thursday. Evidently she has not heard about the storm. The snowplow won't get here till the end of the week.

We went out to see what tracks were about our cabin. The partridge tracks are lovely, a kind of double chain stitch, for the grouse grow snowshoes just as the rabbits do, though theirs are horny projections instead of fluffy pads. Fox and deer have been along the shore, and weasels make two-footed tracks, since, as they bound, their hind feet hit the imprints of the front ones.

The prettiest effect of all is given by the frolicking woodmice. They trace on the snowy surface the most delicate of embroideries, and they have such delight in the process. Woodmice are among the most daring of wild animals, I believe. Not content with scaling tents, here they are dancing gaily across the great open plains of our clearing, where danger is ever present.

The tracks of shrews are even smaller, but not as innocent and inconsequent. They go straight on like a bloodthirsty sentence and come abruptly to a period, when the shrew dives into a snowdrift.

After Lee has scoured the country for snowshoe rabbits—for the rabbit cycle, like the partridge population, is at low ebb this year—we found one living under the empty cabin across the brook. We caught a glimpse of it today, half white and half brown, eating cedar fronds. Its food is supposed to be bark and buds and grass, but that may be because it can't usually reach the cedar; now a fallen tree has made a little bower by the footbridge.

After I was in bed I heard a fox bark, and then the dogs drowned it out; I know we would hear wolves if the dogs weren't so mercurial. For a long time I watched our icicles, which now reach from eaves to snowdrifts, glow incandescent in the moonlit night.

November 11th

We are still isolated from the world, but the snowplow promises to get to us late tonight or sometime tomorrow morning.

36

We all hope it will. Justine Kerfoot called from Duluth this morning, quite perturbed because no one had met her and the children; she hadn't had Bill's wire. And we had all planned to leave Saturday, Arizona and Jack for good, and Lee and I for a week on the North Shore, where we are to meet the Forest Service and see some of their holdings. But it is still uncertain whether the Wilderness Express can get through.

November 12th

The snowplow, late last night, came surging down our drifted hill and landed in front of the lighted lodge, looking like a giant orange butterfly. It is rather a relief to know that now a clear road leads from here to Grand Marais!

Bill has driven to town this morning. We are all looking forward to Justine's arrival with much curiosity. We have heard that she looks like a seventeen-year-old boy, so much so that men are always mistaking her for Bill's son and acting accordingly, that she wears boy's shirts and pants, has a boy's love (and more knowledge than most men have) for motors and machinery, and a skill at profanity which a mere lad would find it difficult to match.

When she graduated from college she had her heart set on becoming a doctor; her mother bought this lodge and handed it over to her as an alternative career. She took that as a challenge and has made herself a real expert in wilderness living. She is an excellent guide, runs hunting and canoe trips, trains the dogs, overhauls motors and equipment. In managing the lodge, Bill takes care of business and she looks after the outdoor angle.

November 13th

Just before dinner last night, Bill and Justine came in with the two children. Justine is slim and dark, quite small. I had expected her to be a tall, husky person. Her hair was cropped short, she wore shirt and trousers, and Lee, coming in late, thought, in spite of all the warnings, that she *was* a boy, and looked around helplessly when Bill introduced him to Justine!

Bruce, almost five, brown eyed and yellow haired, took us in rather soberly. Patty, who is a year and a half, with big brown eyes, a fuzz of brown hair, and a three-cornered smile, paid no attention to us, but immediately attacked the pots and pans, strewing them like seashells in all directions.

Today has been varied. All morning Lee and I packed and fortified the cabin against frost and woodmice. The noon hour was hectic, with all of us milling around between the Indians and trappers who had come for mail. Arizona tried hard to keep the night-club gaiety going to the last, but there were too many hungry babies and heaps of luggage about.

Don, the owner of the Express, was driving today. He and Leo are a great pair, hard-bitten, joking, and nonchalant, but determined that the Express shall run, hell or high snowdrifts; they remind me of what the Pony Express must have been like. We started off at one, Arizona on the seat—I almost said box—with Don. Butchie had tears in her black eyes as she waved good-by.

Today was the first really sunny one for weeks. Clear blue shadows barred the shining roadway hedged with pines. As the sun slanted behind branches, all the snow dimmed to soft blue, with only slits of gold here and there. A beautiful red-gold fox stood like the spirit of this region

38

at a curve of road. He looked a long moment, then made a plumey leap into the deep woods; he curved like a wave—with that fluidity.

Down into Grand Marais the Wilderness Express charged with a stagecoach flourish. After coffee at Mabel's, we dashed at top speed on glare ice to Schroeder, about thirty miles west of Grand Marais.

I had looked at Schroeder as we came out from Duluth, knowing we were to meet the forestry men there. It had a few houses and a combined post office and general store, where we were to stay. I didn't know how I'd like a room over a general store, but Mr. Hendee said it was a comfortable and immaculate place.

It was wonderful! The building was a little gabled one, half store and half home, and when Mrs. Stickney led us upstairs, there was a clean, gay little room, with fresh flowered wallpaper and oh, a modern bathroom! I never saw anything as beautiful as that bathroom! No snow sifting under the door, no windy cracks, no rough boards iced with hoar frost.

We took a sunset walk with traffic in our lives once more. I began to feel very metropolitan, after several cars and a truck came past.

Near by the Cross River crashed down a gorge into the lake, with mist frosting the trees above the chasm. On the shore, as the sunset brightened the water along the little crescent beach, the snowy hills far down the shore turned a soft rosy-mauve, two islands, high chunks of rough rock, stood against a gold glow, and over the water tight flocks of ducks flew low.

The gold changed to coral color, and a flock of snow buntings came eddying over the hill, looking as white as the snowbanks they circled. A little snowstorm, I said to Lee, and he told me the birds *were* sometimes called snowflakes.

On the way back we passed an ancient barn of hand-hewn logs, typical of old Minnesota. This had been a bunkhouse for loggers long ago when logs were sent down this river, until it was found they were so damaged going over the falls that they weren't worth sawing afterward.

After one of Mrs. Stickney's delicious dinners we went down to see Marie Aftreith and Harriet Rust, who run the Star of the North Lodge in summer and drive the school bus in winter. They are living down the road in a friend's house, an attractive white cottage furnished with all modern conveniences.

But, they say, in these severe northern winters it is easier to live primitively. Oil furnace, bathroom, modern kitchen, all these are hazards. If you depend on a wood stove you are sure of fuel. If you carry water from the lake you don't have to worry about pipes freezing. Every convenience means that existence is just that much more complicated in an Arctic climate.

Schroeder, November 14th

Walked down the shore today with Marie Aftreith to see what damage the storm last week had done. At Schroeder it was the worst one since 1905; fishermen's boats were smashed and boathouses, nets, and gear destroyed. Ninety ore carriers were held up in Duluth's harbor.

The fishermen here are very important in our national economy. Along this shore four hundred fishermen in the last two years have made catches totaling twenty million pounds. This last storm was a disaster for many of these men, for the nets and gear are difficult to obtain now and the loss of a house or boat is a heavy blow.

There are no fishing fleets on this shore. The fishermen build their own stout boats, or get a neighbor's help, and go out fishing individually.

40

Occasionally two men go together, but as a rule each fisherman goes alone, in rain, snow, sleet, fog, or hot sun.

The coffee hours, which have become a custom in the North Shore towns, are at eleven and four because the fishermen come in at those hours, tired and cold, sometimes armored in ice. Their mittens get wet and freeze so quickly that they use five or six pairs in one trip, and at times their eyebrows and eyelashes are so thick with ice that they can barely see.

As we walked along the water on the rocks the high waves had washed clear of snow, snow buntings flew before us. Their little tracks were everywhere in the snow. They walk amazing distances through the bronze filigrees of yarrow heads and thistles.

We came to Olaf's log fishhouse, tucked in a hollow between rocks. It is very quaint, one of the oldest on the shore, but he is determined to have a fine new one as soon as possible. This one almost vanished last week when the strong surf swept a great piece of beach out from under it.

Olaf and Dan were in a shed mending nets, which is quite an art. The nets are of fine cord, with a small square mesh dipped in bluestone (a blue vitriol solution) to preserve them. When they come out they are a beautiful Madonna blue, though they turn rust color as they are used.

These are gill nets, and they are anchored by bags of sand and buoyed either by quart-size whisky bottles (which are used now instead of the former picturesque glass balls) or by plastic capsules, which have taken the place of cork buoys.

The catch is mostly herring, which is not really herring at all but is related to the whitefish. Whitefish and ciscoes are caught sometimes, though they are rare on this coast. The lake trout are caught on setlines, and since these have to be twelve or more miles from shore, the fishermen who specialize in trout receive gasoline allotments accordingly.

Tall, blue-eyed Olaf from Norway took us out to show us how his boat is landed. On the rocky shore the boat comes up on a slide, a wide lattice of poles. The man leaps out and hitches a line to it so it can be pulled into the boathouse by a windlass. His leap, when rocks and poles are icy, is often a perilous one. Back of the slide stands the fishhouse and a big square rack on which the nets are wound and dried.

This afternoon we walked to Temperance River, so called, they told us, because it is the only river along the shore without a bar at its mouth. It seems the wildest of all the North Shore rivers, for its white water tears through a black gorge so narrow that it is only a jagged crack splitting deeply through the cliff. Its walls were hung with screens of long icicles, and gigantic chunks of crystals bulged from the froth of water. As we climbed the cliff the trail of an enormous buck went before us, and a mink had just crossed the footbridge at the top of the gorge. On an isolated pinnacle we saw the footmarks of a reckless and melancholy partridge.

November 16th

Mr. Jacobs of the Forest Service took us with him today on his rounds—a fascinating day he gave us. I had hoped for mild weather, but it was two above zero—the coldest we've had. However, a bright sun counterbalanced the low temperature.

We went first to the Tofte ranger station, a collection of fine log buildings, an office, a storehouse, and rangers' homes. In the office were regional maps of all kinds and sizes, and here we lost all track of time. The airplane photographs, which give three dimensions through a stereopticon device, delighted us. We hovered over the Gunflint region, finding paths and heights, even recognizing tiny individual trees. One map had pegs that showed at once where each ranger was; one showed areas ripe for supervised cutting, another outlined present lumbering. For use in fighting forest fires, a map was marked in terms of the time it takes to arrive at any given area—up to ten hours in the most remote districts.

We saw the storehouses for the fire equipment too, and appreciated the vigorous foresight shown here. Each unit had a complete working outfit for the number of men it was to supply. The cans stood already packed with all necessary food and supplies, even to an alarm clock for waking the cook! Sleeping bags, blankets, life preservers, were stored carefully in mouse-proofed cupboards. And everything was so arranged that it could be seized without one moment's loss of time.

Mr. Jacobs told us that during the season when forest fires are most likely to occur, there are men in twenty-five lookout towers. Hydroplanes too are used. Any fire can be reported at once, and emergency equipment is kept in red boxes along principal trails and canoe routes. The reduction of the fire hazard is most remarkable, though there is still great danger from careless campers. The Service says, "Five minutes spent in extinguishing a campfire, or even one minute devoted to

stamping out a cigarette, may be the
equivalent of a hundred years of forest growth."

Afterward we drove up the Sawbill Road, which follows the Temperance River. It was even colder away from the lake, and heavy frost
clung thick to branches and twigs and gave a curious sparkle to the
blue air. Deer vaulted in airy crescents across our way.

We turned off on a logging road to Moe's Camp, where pine timber
had been sold by the Forest Service to the highest bidder. The day of
the huge sawmills is now largely over; most of the lumber in Minnesota
is being cut by portable mills.

A small one was working at this camp. Two men rolled the big
pine logs with cant hooks onto a movable carriage. As the logs traveled
along, they were cut into boards by a circular saw. In this case the slabs
and bark, as well as the boards, were being marketed. In the large mills

44

the sawdust is used for fuel under the boilers, but in these portable mills the power is the tractor, or a Diesel motor.

The men worked with great skill and swiftness here. Lumberjacks were skidding logs to the mill in various ways, using horses and a pair of tongs, or the caterpillar tractor. I wanted to see a go-devil, liking the name, but no such sled was around this camp.

We went scrambling over fallen pines with their beautiful branches hidden in the snow, and the noise of the sawmill was loud about us. Suddenly a tall pine trembled in front of us and fell with a crash just across our path. We were almost under it. A Norwegian was sawing immediately before us, in a clump of dense spruce, and had not heard us coming. He worked as so many of these men do, alone, at his own tempo, and was paid by the amount of timber he cut.

A flock of pine siskins came by us and lit in a gnarled tree. I have had a fondness for siskins ever since I read that these midget gypsies distract ornithologists by their unorthodox behavior. Peabody says flatly that they are eccentric, and Dr. Roberts accuses them of junketing winter and summer and of rearing their families in most unconventional places. "Throughout the spring and summer," he says sternly, "when they should be paired and nesting, flocks wander about apparently with no intention of settling down to home making."

While we watched these small birds, the dinner bell rang and the men began to converge on the camp. But as the cook had asked us to wait till the second table, we went on through the pines. This was the most closely grown white pine we had seen anywhere, beautiful stately trees, and I mourned their destruction. Mr. Jacobs said they were far past their prime, as was shown by the number of rotting centers. Just the same, I thought rebelliously, it takes two hundred years before we can see trees like these; I'd let the old giants stand until they dropped.

Out in the cutting the ground was so covered with fallen trees that we had to walk on crisscross logs, my big boots making me less a gazelle than I could have wished. After these logs are cut the tops and branches are piled and burned, even under heavy snow, and I wish that we could have seen these great bonfires in the snowy woods. We found a ranger in this jackstraw pile, stamping "U. S." with a hammer on the log ends and marking the number of board feet in a scale record book.

Lunch at the camp was like harvest home. Ham and spareribs and beef and chile, potatoes and gravy and peas and rolls, cakes, cookies, custard pudding. The cook said that he never lost a lumberjack. "They keep coming back year after year. Money don't mean so much; they only get out once in a long while to spend it. But meals come three times a day and they're the most important thing to a logger!"

After lunch we drove to other timber stands. A white pine forest not yet cut. Cheerful areas where the foresters had planted red pines and the white pines had started themselves—flourishing young forests, exciting to see. A great spruce stand, cut over so expertly that we could not tell the cut areas from the uncut ones, stood dense and dark, with tiny snow triangles dotted up and down the black trunks and branches, an allover design in three dimensions.

On one hill where old white pines were left standing here and there for seeding, the young trees had made such successful progress that the old ones could now be cut. This cutting is always done in winter with snow on the ground, when the damage to young trees is slightest.

We drove down rough logging roads, impassable swamps in summer, but now hard-packed and easy to drive over. The shadows were growing darker now, and a clear yellow light shone far beyond the woods. A porcupine with a grumpy little face wallowed off the road into deep snow.

We walked down a trail through heavy jackpine and spruce, and in a snowy hollow we came on the porcupine's den in an overturned stump. I have never seen anything more disarming. The way the snow lay on the stump it seemed a perfect tiny cottage. One root made a ridgepole, others made drooping eaves, and snow. drifted the steep roof and a little lean-to. The small doorway, almost square, was hung with green vines, and a green doorsill shone brilliant with moss where the porcupine had scraped away the snow. I almost expected to see WELCOME on that mat.

Here Mr. Jacobs showed us how the Swedish increment borer is used to determine the age of trees and therefore the selection of stands to be cut. It is a fascinating little instrument, a drill which takes a core like a thin pencil from a living tree, so that the forester, by counting the rings and observing their width, can tell if the annual growth has decreased to such an extent that it is no longer economical to delay cutting. One healthy spruce was seventy years old, and a sound pine was one hundred and seventy. In this area much of the timber is ripe while still rather small.

The jackpines, the rangers say, *need* fire for reseeding. The fire opens the cones and permits the seeds to reach the mineral soil. The red pine is less successful than the white pine in reseeding itself, for the solid carpet of needles insulates the seed from the earth. This is why the squirrels are so necessary as foresters; in storing cones they shove them down through the needles into the ground.

Next we saw some lumbering on private land. Here the destruction was complete. They were cutting eight-inch spruce and jackpine into dimension stuff, and all species were cut. The contrast between the lumbering here and that on the supervised areas made us feel very enthusiastic about the work done by the Forest Service.

November 17th

Mr. Hendee, chief of the Forest Service here, joined us today, and after visiting the forest headquarters again we took the Caribou Lake Road. Here was a small and picturesque sawmill run by an old Negro and his family, with the help of a few Norwegians. This is the only colored family on the North Shore, and they hold a respected place in the community. Their summer resort is one of the neatest and cleanest in the whole region.

The timber was varied, and in places where the cutting was finished many trees were still standing—large birches, spruces, even tall white pines—so that the area had no look of devastation. The Forest Service, Mr. Hendee says, cuts only dead or dying trees within two hundred feet of any road, so that visually an area is not changed by logging.

Mr. Hendee believes that a managed area with reasonable cutting and good fire protection will give a better forest than one in which no cutting is done. That is true, I'm sure, for Mr. Hendee has studied these problems thoroughly, but I *still* like my wilderness untouched!

As Mr. Jacobs was showing us trees whose trunks had been cracked wide open by intense cold and had later healed over, we heard a sound of tearing and ripping in a thicket. Then a pileated woodpecker plunged up a pine. Every feather of his wild scarlet crest blazed in the sun. The white streak slanting through his eye, the black band up his neck, and his breastplate of coarse iron-gray, more like hair than feathers, made him look like the pirate of the bird kingdom.

He made great *lunges* up the tree. Not hops; it takes a light bird to hop, and he weighed as much as a ruffed grouse. On the pine tip he looked around challengingly, gave a whoop, and flew galloping away. He seemed the most untamed creature I ever saw; certainly far more impressive than that bear we encountered.

Back to Lake Superior, we drove down past Two Island River to Sugar Loaf Landing, where pulpwood is piled in unbelievable amounts. Row after row of wood piled high, and many times as much to come. Next summer the logs will be floated in rafts across Lake Superior to the Wisconsin mills.

The men at work here wore gay plaid shirts, and a little yellow tractor buzzed out into the shallow water and up on the shore, bringing in logs that had washed away in last week's storm. Luckily the gale blew from the east, so the logs stayed in this bay, but they were churned and beaten until the ends looked chewed as if by mammoth beavers. If the wind had shifted many thousands of these logs would have been lost.

Schroeder, November 17th

Last night we met Mr. Aldous of the Fish and Wildlife Service, who is also staying here, and he told us tales of a baby porcupine his children had adopted. I have wanted a pet flying squirrel, but he almost made me long for a small porcupine instead. This one became a real pet, playful and affectionate, though not to be cuddled with impunity.

He asked us to go with him today on a survey of the deer yards in this vicinity. These are sheltered places with coniferous growth where the deer gather when the snowfalls have been heavy. When fires have destroyed much forest growth there is great overcrowding here. Mr. Aldous has fenced off experimental areas to determine how much browsing various plants suitable for deer food will stand, and today he was making an inspection tour.

The trees were frosty white against a shell-pink sky as we started out in the early morning. We went up the trail to Onion Mountain through rather open country, once burned over. In a saddle we found the deer yard, a tangled cedar swamp. Later in the day we visited the Jonvik yard east of Lutsen. That was eight miles long, on a wet slope where the trickles of water beneath the snow made me glad of my boots. Through the dense growth of small balsam and cedars and the little open glades with overbrowsed brush, we found the tracks, sharply incised, which showed where deer had been recently feeding, though there were no great concentrations as yet. The most heavily used runway went across a footbridge high over the Cascade River!

The white-tailed deer is a Johnny-Come-Lately in this part of Minnesota. Here caribou once ranged and moose were found in great numbers. It was only after the first lumbering and the subsequent forest fires that deer came in to replace moose, which are now much less

50

numerous. During the lumbering the new growth suitable for deer food increased rapidly, and there was temporarily a great abundance of winter food, as deer ate at night the tops of the trees cut during the day.

We walked along the runways the deer had made. These runways are made in the early snows and kept open. Mr. Aldous said that the deer seem unwilling or unable to break through heavy drifts, and they will not leave these trails even though food may be found only a short distance away. He has discovered that the deer will not even pass from one yard to another unless the two are connected by at least a thin line of evergreens, and so he has planted a few trees, as an experiment, to connect two areas and lead the deer along.

We saw traces of a fierce and bloody fight between two bucks on one hillside, and in a green thicket we came on a freshly killed fawn which, except for head and skin, had been entirely eaten by foxes and ravens. Tracks showed where the ravens had frequently walked to a small brook near by for water. Mr. Aldous said that the herring gulls too come down in heavy woods to feed on dead deer.

"Do many deer die of starvation?" I asked.

"We've found," said Mr. Aldous, "that in the worst years the loss of deer through starvation about equals the kill by hunters. But the situation may become worse than that."

"I wonder if the wolves don't have their role in the balanced wilderness," said Lee. "I doubt the virtues of the bounty system and the effort to exterminate them. Of course, I *like* them. Wolves and moose give character to the wilderness!"

"And pileated woodpeckers," I added, thinking of the pirate we saw yesterday.

"Yes, and the spruce grouse," Lee said. "Those four mean untamed country. But of them all the wolf is the shyest."

"Darling!" I said, enraptured, "now you have really reached the depths of understatement! It takes you to call a wolf shy!"

We had noticed, on many lake shores in this region a perfectly straight line made by the browsing deer, which eat all cedar fronds as high as they can reach. Mr. Aldous said the deer are especially fond of the white cedar, and that it is the only evergreen which alone will sustain them.

But as the cedar, once stripped, fails to replace its leaves, one can see that this source of food is rapidly diminishing.

In early winter the deer eat, besides cedar, the new growth on the deciduous brush, preferring dogwood and moose or mountain maple. Later in the winter they are forced to eat more and more balsam, which is abundant but not nourishing enough to keep the deer strong and healthy.

As we drove back down the North Shore, Mr. Aldous told us that as the snow thaws first on these southern slopes facing Lake Superior, the deer come in great numbers to feed here in the early spring, and sometimes as many as two hundred may be seen from the highway.

Gunflint, November 20th

Today the five-day hunting season on deer opened. Hunters were coming by all night. This year they are required to wear outfits that are fifty per cent red, and we hear that there is no red material in the towns now—every bit has been bought by hunters.

When we caught the Wilderness Express for Gunflint it was packed with excited men and boys, and the road along Lake Superior was like a brilliant poster, with scarlet-clad hunters, white snow, and green pines. This is really an invasion by an army—a jovial army, but rather an over-powering sight just the same. Many are real sportsmen, but some have no idea that a gun is a dangerous weapon, and there are always tragic accidents.

Grand Marais was in carnival, and when we turned into the Gun-flint Trail the woods were vivid with dotted red figures, wearing every-thing from an entire hunting suit of scarlet to a casual bandana or strips of cerise corduroy stretched across a burly back. One ferocious hunter

53

with a three-day growth of black whiskers wore a delicate baby-pink suede jacket.

We reached the lodge in late afternoon. All the lakes on the way are frozen over now, but Gunflint Lake is so deep it is still open. The lodge is filled with hunters, from a party of young naval officers to a cowboy radio singer and his wife. Deer are already hanging from the porch, and Bruce and the dogs are wild with excitement.

November 21st

Lee had insisted all along that it would be foolish for him to get a fifty-dollar nonresident hunting license; after all, he had hunted enough when he was a boy. But as the season approached his resistance waned and all he needed was a little persuasion. Finally he didn't need that.

I had thought it would be exciting to go deer hunting with him. But I discovered this morning that I'd decided not to go, which is a surprise to both of us. I certainly don't feel opposed to it. Since there are sometimes too many deer for the available winter food supply it is better for them to be shot than to starve. Men get a great thrill from the hunting and now there is a real need for meat. But I am a traitor in this camp; I am the underground. I don't like to see dead deer.

When we went to the lodge for breakfast, some hunters were scouting along the shore, others going to stands along the ski trail. A telephone call told us that two hunters had been shot on the North Shore, one killed outright and one fatally wounded. Suddenly all the scarlet costumes were no longer comedy; it was a matter of life and death.

Justine, with Butchie's help, has everything to do, for Bill is out all day with the hunters. She has twenty-five people to feed, and this morning the water system had stopped, the pipes frozen, and the light plant broke down. She repaired them, one after another, besides cleaning a dozen chickens, making pies and cakes, and baking bread. I gasp at what goes on behind the scenes. When you're a guest you take it so as a matter of course that everything goes like clockwork.

The men take their lunches with them, but it's very cold, and all day long they are in and out for coffee and snacks, telling tales of their adventures. The baby is into the silver, throwing it across the

floor as fast as it is collected, or dipping into the pail of dog food with a slipper. Bruce on his velocipede wheels joyfully through the melee.

As I didn't go out on the battle line this morning, I helped in the kitchen, where dishes pile up in mountainous heaps. This afternoon I walked as far as the Trail with Lee, who likes to hunt by himself and takes a different direction from the main march. He had a red plaid jacket, a red hunting cap, and my red scarf. So I wore the scarlet pareu with the white splashy flowers which I have been using as a table cover, wrapping it around me like a large shawl. A South Sea sarong may be rather incongruous in zero weather, but it doesn't look like a deer.

November 22d

The lake was as still as glass as we went over to breakfast, snowy hills doubled in the water, and rising mist half hid the clear pastel colors of the morning. The porch thermometer showed three below zero.

When we came into the kitchen we found that Justine, hurriedly cutting big slices of ham, had slashed her hand to the bone. Just the same, she was getting breakfast for thirty. She certainly does nobly with the cooking, which she had always ignored until Aggie was hurt this summer. She hates "women's work," but this is a job to be done; I've already learned that when there's a challenge she meets it, work or play.

This morning Butchie helped with the kitchen work and cooking (for Justine could use only one hand), as well as looking after all the cabins and the livestock. So I took over the dishes. I don't know how a mere breakfast can stack up so; I washed dishes all morning, just as fast as I could. Butchie and I had a quick game of double solitaire before lunchtime caught us.

The radio cowboy, who had never hunted deer before, was determined to take one back. Since he had to leave today he hunted until noon, then gave up in despair. But as he turned to come home, at the last possible second, a deer came through the swamp and he got his prize.

Later Lee came in. Quietly, but I knew he was excited. He had just shot a buck back on the ridge, the biggest one that has been shot here.

Bill went out with him to drag it in, and later Bruce and I walked up the road to meet them, I wrapped in my gay pareu and Bruce with his mother's red plaid shirt for an overcoat, a big red cap with wide ear flaps, and stumpy little boots. He looked cute and crazy, rather like Disney's Dopey, except for his fresh, rosy little face.

He is my favorite north woods guide, and *very* knowledgeable. He showed me tracks of deer and rabbit. "We snared a big rabbit last winter—three inches long!" he said, his eyes wide and earnest. But he does not often make a mistake. His woodlore is astounding, and whatever he knows he remembers in clear-cut pictures—no fuzzy, vague conceptions for Bruce.

One of the Navy men lost his bearings up on the hills tonight, but the howling of the sled dogs brought him safely to port. Three men who took a boat down the lake with Indian guides brought in two does and a fawn. All the hunters were in high spirits tonight and high with spirits too. Over and over they told how they got their deer, till I felt as if they had turned into so many parrots. Far into the night, mirth and song wafted through the woods from lighted cabins.

November 23d

I walked up the ridge with Lee, to see the spot where he had shot his buck, through a beautiful zero morning with hoar frost deep on the trees. In my ski suit, hood, mittens, and boots, with no cracks at wrists or neck, I am like my own little house. I take off my mittens to get cool, as you'd open a window.

We went through a silver world with a turquoise sky around us. Up the ridge in the shadow, the frost was blue in the air like smoke, and on the crest the trees were frosted till they looked wrapped in white fur.

The jackpines were all a shining silver, every tiny needle, not dark green and white as they are in snow, and huge frost crystals as wide as my thumb-nail tilted on the snow surface.

The distances were rosy and faint lavender. Though the sun was low along the south hills all day, it shone warm on the ridge top, and the frost glinted in the air, falling around us in a light shower. The frosty trees in the valleys looked like white clouds resting there.

Pine siskins looped through the poplars, which swayed purest white against the deep blue above them. We came upon two deer so absorbed in eating poplar leaves from a dead tree that we walked up almost on them before they dashed off in wild panic.

On our evening walk we found pine grosbeaks. A male, a radiant rose with strongly marked wing feathers, and females or immature birds of soft gray with orange on their heads and backs. They flew from one spruce top to another; their sweet, clear notes are the only real melody we have heard in the winter woods.

Thanksgiving

Raining, snowing, sleeting.

Now the country is left to its few residents; the hunters have gone. The Kerfoots moved up into their own cottage on the hill today and shut up the main lodge. Butchie went home. Lee says "no more playing"; he is settling down to his work.

The moving took all day, and we just skipped Thanksgiving. I felt

58

a little homesick for the lodge kitchen and Butchie tonight. The low, log cottage, which Bill and Justine built themselves, is just right for two people, but the kitchen is very cramped for six, especially when two of them make up in speed and sound for what they lack in size! In the only clear space in the center of the room is a trapdoor, which leads down into the root cellar and furnace room, and through which Justine and Bill are always disappearing and reappearing, like distraught magicians.

Tonight Lee was taking measurements of his buck's head—he wants to make a wood carving of it—and Justine was cutting up a frozen doe in the cold kitchen of the lodge. Justine got a great kick out of the intricate measurements and calculations Lee made so that the carving would have the exact proportions of the deer. Lee says it was quite a sight to see Justine, meat cleaver in hand, throw herself at that doe!

But Justine, in spite of her liking for rigorous activities, isn't at all masculine. Her boyishness is more an urchin's—a gamin quality. She is very gentle with the children, and then the next minute she is perched on a chair back, talking as gruff and rough as any old trapper she is conversing with. But I'm beginning to have a dark suspicion that she is really a very sensitive person, tenderhearted and beauty loving, though she would die rather than admit it.

Butchie is starting off tomorrow to set her beaver traps. The beaver season is open in Ontario, though not in Minnesota. Butchie traps all winter. She has her own territory and trapping shack, as most of the Chippewas do. The canned supplies at these camps are kept from freezing by putting them in a gunny sack and lowering them into the water under the ice, where they stay above freezing temperature. In the old days cranberries were stored in baskets and kept till spring in this way.

Butchie's cousin, Charlie Cook, is here to cut dead birches and aspens for wood this winter. The swing of his axe, so effortless and effective, is as beautiful to watch as dancing. Now I see why Lee groans when he sees our city laborers chopping at trees.

I wish the Indians would use their Chippewa names; Charlie doesn't look at all like Charlie Cook! There used to be two ancient Indian women who lived across the lake in a birch-bark wigwam—Mrs. Spruce and Mrs. Tamarack.

Bits of snowstorms all day. The rabbit that lives next door is all white now with black eartips, trying to be an ermine. We have wondered why he did not wander away, but it seems that each rabbit has his own little territory. Sometimes one may stay a whole season within a radius of a hundred yards.

The woodmice are living in our woodbox now. One took over the top dresser drawer till I found him there and gave him a scornful look that drove him out. I am almost sorry, for it is amazing to have a wild animal live in your dresser drawer, and he *is* wild, as wild as a deer, and very cunning with his big ears and bright eyes and immaculate white vest and stockings.

Now the little creatures only scurry out at night, and they eat the queerest things, the soap wrappings, the white flowers out of my blue Swiss scarf, the brim of Lee's hat. One fell in the water pitcher, and Lee poured him out from the spout; he came forth looking very meek. I did not mind even that very much, they are such clean, woodsy little things.

November 28th

Mail day! I can't begin to say how exciting mail is when it comes only once a week! People begin to arrive by breakfast time; the house gets fuller and fuller till it spills over. Today the Blankenburgs came in from Saganaga.

They tried to find us the day we went to Schroeder, to join their bear hunt! At first I felt extremely disappointed to have missed it. The bear was one that had annoyed them all summer, and last week when Mr. B. found its den in the rocks he poked his head in, pushing it almost into the bear's face! Then they organized a bear hunt.

Half a dozen of them lined up with their rifles and Mr. B. poked the bear with a pole. It had to be prodded and peppered before it would even wake up. Finally one paw came forth from the cave's mouth, and then the bear stumbled out, half asleep and blinking, to be shot. I am rather glad now that we were not there.

Lee has begun a panorama of Gunflint Lake from the hilltop we climbed the other morning. It was too cold to sketch there—he almost froze his hand—but he made a few notes and is drawing from those.

November 30th

After more snow it is warm again, and Justine and I decided to walk to the cliff top. Bruce begged to go along. He seemed very small to wade through the drifts we would find, but I remembered the stalwart way he hiked down the Trail with me. Justine, agreeing he could go, got out the tikinagan, the Indian cradleboard.

Patty, wrapped in blankets, was laid on the board, two deerskin flaps folded over her, and then she was laced in. Justine hoisted the board to her back, slipped her arms through shoulder straps (the Indians use a headband, called a tumpline), and we started out.

We were all in high spirits at the crisp, sunny day, Bruce so delighted that he babbled like our brook from the time we started till we got back. Patty was silent, except when she got too large a faceful of snow from hanging branches as we climbed the trail.

When Justine saw a porcupine furrow she followed that up a steep and snowy slope, to where the beast had climbed straight up a rock face to its den. There she stuck Patty's tikinagan in the snow and skinned up the wall like a wildcat to the mouth of the den, where she balanced on a knob of root. "This is a darn nice den," she called.

"I want to see!" said Bruce. Justine swung herself over a ledge, and Bruce got himself up, clinging and clutching. I didn't see how I could possibly follow; with my mammoth boots I had no way of getting toeholds. But if Bruce went, who was I to hang back? So up I went, terrified when I reached the knob and there was nothing to clutch. The den was a nice one, as dens go, with two rooms and a bath down the hill.

We all reached the high ledge by clinging to roots and twigs, in which I had no faith, and then Justine went down a less precipitous way to pick up Patty. After that we climbed the "little cliff," which gives a wonderful view of lake and narrows and white hills.

Spruce branches against brilliant blue and clouds of creamy lavender tossed around us. Far off and far below on an ice-covered bay we could see a tiny figure crossing the ice on skis.

Bruce's mittens were soaked with snow and we were warm from the climb, so we moved out of the wind into a snowy hollow, where we built a fire and hung our mittens up to dry. Patty yelled loudly until she was stuck in the drifts facing the fire, which flamed orange and vivid in the snow. Justine cut heaps of spruce boughs for cushions, and we sat there comfortably with squares of chocolate for afternoon tea. Branches, snow-laden, hung like curtains around us.

"I never dreamed I could *relax* outdoors in winter weather," I said lazily.

"The whole thing is to play *with* the weather, not fight it," Justine said. "If it's calm, we go out on the lake, if it's windy we go back in the woods. You see, we were chilled through on the cliff edge, but here it's all right.

"Another thing, people often wear winter clothes that are too tight. They need loose, light wool things and windbreakers that are loppy. The skin needs to breathe. Lots of layers are far better than heavy garments. When boots or rubber pacs are too cold we wear moccasins with lots of stockings. Often I do chores in my stocking feet if the snow is dry, and the layers of wool insulate me against the cold."

Bruce's mittens were nearly dry and he dropped them in the fire, so we fished them out and started home.

"We'll take another trail down," Justine said, and started through the spruces. A dark cliff hung over us. Under the trees we saw sheltered beds where deer had lain, the snow flattened and worn away till the green moss shone through. We came to an edge of cliff that dropped straight down. "This is one place we won't go down," I said cheerfully. So we did.

Justine dropped over the edge with the baby on her back, swinging from one slim trunk to another, but Bruce and I slid, he with yips of delight and I with a qualm at first and then with utter abandon. It was as much fun as tobogganing, only now I was sliding straight down from tree to tree without a sled.

We scrambled rowdily on down through spruces, leaping and plunging as we liked, for the snowdrifts were sure to catch us. Halfway up the huge trunk of a white pine we saw a hole, freshly chiselled, made by a pileated woodpecker—one of the rare birds that make themselves winter domiciles.

64

All the resort owners seem to take to trapping in the winter, though they keep their amateur status. Bill went off before daylight to start his winter trapping line. He has a shack over on Bruce Lake, seven miles or so from here, and he departed on snowshoes with thirty-two steel traps, blankets, grub, utensils, repair outfit, and cans of rotten fish for lure (not allure) hung all over him. "Just a touch overweight," he said. Justine says he must have been carrying a hundred pounds.

I went down the ski trail this morning. Nine ravens circled overhead, croaking and creaking. Two came by together, cooing in guttural affection. Then they made odd liquid clucking notes which they varied with shrill cries. These northern ravens, far wilder birds than eagles, delight in winter living, and are found around the globe in Arctic countries. At one time it was feared they were vanishing from Minnesota, but we have seen them often this year.

Justine has decided she must get the dogs in training. They have not been driven since last winter. She hitched three dogs today—Swede, a

65

natural lead dog, intelligent and dependable, but small and overconscientious; Whittles, the beauty, young and inexperienced; and Egi-guk, a magnificent white Malamute from Alaska, trained as wheel dog.

She got out the dog sled, which is very flexible and light, for a rigid sled would break under the strain on these rough trails. Then she unchained Whittles from the lodge porch and, snapping his chain to the sled, helped him pull it up the hill to the dog kennels.

Clamor broke loose. Such barking and howling and the wild, long wail—so wonderful to hear—from Egi-guk! All the dogs bounding in the air and straining at their chains—I never saw such fierce, flaming looks!

Justine gave me Whittles's chain to hold, while she fastened the sled to a stout post and then got Whittles's harness on him. Half crazy with excitement, he kept getting his chain around my feet as he whirled. The noise was beyond bounds. These loud-voiced furies, leaping into the air, were far from my idea of tamed animals, but I liked watching Justine with them, she was so intent and efficient.

Swede's harness on, he was unchained and snapped on the lead rope in front of Whittles. There he pulled forward, straining ahead and letting out one bark after another, like a car horn that had stuck.

Egi went completely mad when he found he was to go. Egi's whole pride is in going in the team. Once when he was unruly they took him off the sled. The punishment nearly broke his heart, and he has been dependable ever since. When he is left behind he chews down saplings in his tumultuous despair.

The harnessed dogs, leaping about, tangled their pull ropes, but they did not fight. Justine straightened them out, got the sled in deep snow, and unsnapped the sled chain from the post. Bruce screamed, "Justee-an! I want to go!" So she slung him on the sled, grabbed the handles in back, and called "Mush!"

The dogs started. Rather slowly, surprisingly, but the snow was deep. They dragged down the hill into the road. There they dashed off over the east hill. I walked after them after ordering Ginger back to her puppies; she was all for following and making trouble. The team came back over the hill in orderly fashion.

"Want a ride?" Justine asked.

I sat down in the sled. The supports ran high on each side, so there

66

was no way of tumbling off voluntarily if our steeds ran away. Bruce sat on my lap. Justine called to the dogs and we started off. It was delightful, like mild tobogganing. The dogs paced along steadily—brown back, black-and-cream back, white back, with fluffed waving tails, ahead of us. Justine, riding on the rear runners or trotting beside the dogs, encouraged them constantly. "That's the boy, Swede! Good work, Egi. Keep it up, Whittles!"

We swooped downhill, the sled hitting Egi's heels, the dogs going faster and faster, then slowed to a walk on the upgrade.

"Gosh, I'm proud of Whittles!" Justine said. "He's really working. I didn't think he had it in him."

The dogs were still joyous, but they grew tired before long. On a long hill they would go more and more slowly till they came to a stop, then look around to see why Justine didn't order them ahead.

Swede led the team to either side of the road at Gee or Haw, but when Justine wanted to turn them around and called, "Haw! Back!" they were confused, and that we had to practice. Justine says that a dog behind the lead shows qualifications for leadership when he learns Gee and Haw himself, instead of following the leader.

We went up a long hill. The dogs ate snow when we let them rest, but they weren't panting hard. The day cleared, and big, creamy clouds shouldered up over the bare treetops. It was exhilarating to dash down the hill again. "If they just don't see a deer, we're O.K.," Justine said. "And Whittles is going to be *all right!*"

Back toward the kennels, the other dogs set up their usual clamor, intensified, and our team came in docilely. Swede, good little Swede, was worn out; he lay down in the snow before his house. But Egi stood up proudly on the roof of his kennel and howled with pride.

Lee asked Just at supper what hitch she used. "We used to use double traces," she said, "but the dogs don't have much freedom that way, and we lost a dog once when the team broke through the ice. So now we use a center rope with the dogs' harness clipped to it. Each dog is pretty much on his own that way, and you can see if anyone is a slacker. There's another hitch used in the Arctic, where each dog pulls on a rope directly from the sled, but that would never work in the woods."

"When did you break through the ice?" I asked her.

"Oh, we were on a camping trip and the dogs ran away and the ice broke under them. I went out to get them and broke through too. Then Bill came out to get me. He wriggled out flat on the ice and got hold of me, but I wouldn't let go of the dogs and he couldn't get us all out. Instead, *he* went in! Then he broke ice till his feet hit bottom, got his footing, and pulled us all ashore. But the dogs had been struggling all the time and one was pushed under and drowned. Yes, it was pretty cold weather; we had quite a time drying out."

It is below zero at night. It seems as natural now to take our snowy path from the cottage through the dark woods to our cabin as to go down our own hallway in New York. Tonight the thin ice along the shore made little tinkling sounds, like the glass windbells that used to ring on summer nights in our porch at home, and a crescent moon was hung just over our chimney.

December 3d

A south wind this morning! Our lake will never freeze at this rate, and we want to *see* it freeze over.

This afternoon with the dogs was not the complete triumph we scored yesterday. Justine took the other three, all inexperienced, with Gus as leader. I mistrusted Gus. He's a big yellow brute with black triangles for eyes, and he looks devil-ridden and shifty. I thought firmly to myself, "*Nothing* will induce me to go out with him."

Wolf next. The most unlike a wolf of any of the dogs, he is gentle and unassuming. Loppy was wheel dog; he is quiet but his eyes have a fanatical look. The team didn't compare with yesterday's.

As they were being harnessed, Gus kept growling in his throat, while the others looked apprehensive.

"Are you going?" Bruce asked me.

"Not today," I said.

"I won't either."

"Florence, will you be ballast," Justine called, "while I get them down to the road?" So on I climbed; Bruce hopped in beside me.

We started with a violent jerk, flew through the snow, and swerved into the road. The next thing I knew I was trying to get my head above a snowdrift. Bruce was intact, the sled lay upside down, the three dogs were one snarling, furious mass, and Justine was beating them with a heavy stick.

I was frightened. I'd never seen a real dog fight, and this one was far too fierce and bloody. Justine grabbed Gus by the collar and threw him toward us—quite a feat for a small person, but she is made of steel spring. I was still tangled in the sled and I feared Gus would mistake me for another dog and start a fight with me. Bruce was up, half crying, half enthralled. Gus leaped back into the fray, but Justine kicked him away and hauled Loppy off.

Wolf lay still on the snow. I thought he was dead, but Justine patted him and encouraged him till he got on his feet again. Loppy's harness broke and he ran away. We all took a deep breath and looked at one another.

"Not so good a start," Justine said.

She lined Wolf up behind Gus. "I'll see what the pair of them can do." She started them down the road, Bruce and I following. Then Loppy appeared on the crest of the hill.

"Can you hold these two a minute?" Justine asked me. "If they start to run, jump on the back runners." Oh yes, I thought, and then I'll be going along for the ride. Fine!

However, I held on, while Justine sauntered up to Loppy and got her hands on his harness. Then she hauled him by main force back to the sled. "My heavens, she's going on with it," I realized.

"Look, F.," she said, "will you sit in the sled till I get them going?"

I looked at Gus. "All right," I said, and sat down. "I want to go," Bruce decided. "Climb aboard," Justine called. "Mush!"

Nothing happened. Gus growled and Loppy gazed dreamily at the landscape. "You ornery pups!" Justine shouted, "Get goin'!" No response.

"Damn fools!" Justine muttered. "Come on, you!" She started downhill and they followed, Gus veering perversely and Wolf leaning like a faded flower.

"By the livin' jimmies, what a sight!" Just cried. She ran down the road and they followed. Loppy tangled in his harness for the third time, and Justine made Wolf wheel dog. No sooner did she put Loppy second than he and Gus flew at each other. Just grimly relined them as they were before.

"Mush now," she yelled. They didn't bother to look around. "Mush, you blazin' hounds!" She ran ahead. It was bitterly cold. Bruce and I looked for tracks in the snow, but it was hard to take an interest when the last thing we wanted to see just now was a deer. Finally the sled turned around and we struggled back again.

Suddenly it was different. Gus's tail was up at an arrogant angle, the cockiest curl I ever saw, and he was stepping. Wolf was trotting along steadily, and Loppy was going so well that the sled didn't strike his legs. "Good dogs! Now you're loggin'! Yippee!" We went sailing home.

December 4th

Bill is still away and Lee is deep in picturing a fight between two bucks. He took a half day off this afternoon and we walked to the beaver pond. Justine took yesterday's dogs out again, for it is necessary to drive the dogs regularly to toughen them. Bruce, and Patty in her tikinagan, went along. Patty did fall upside down off the sled, but the headbar on the tikinagan caught her and she wasn't hurt. Gus threatened Justine a couple of times, something no other dog has ever done.

December 5th

Justine, Bruce, and I set up a trap line and rabbit snares today. I hope Bill won't resent us, as the early trappers did their rivals. Alexander Henry wrote in 1775, "At the Grand Portage, I found the fur traders in a state of extreme reciprocal hostility, each pursuing his interests in such a manner as might most injure his neighbor."

We went along the black brook through the snowy cedar swamp. Ginger and the puppies, determined to join the expedition, were difficult to discourage.

Justine set the first trap where she found a mink's tracks crossing the brook. Anchoring the trap to a log, she stuck a stick through a frozen herring and into the ground. Then she built a little cubby over it against the tree trunk, with sticks set close together, on each side, so that a mink could enter only from the front. Balsam boughs were woven through the sticks.

Next she made a rabbit snare, a loop of thin wire with a running knot, which dangled from a low branch and was spread out by thin twigs, in a rabbit's runway. It is delicate work to arrange the twigs so that they will keep the circle open and yet not interfere with the loop when it draws tight.

Justine bounded back and forth across the brook like a rabbit, and Bruce fell into so many holes I told him he was a holey terror, but he struggled on undaunted, even crossing the brook on logs hidden in deep snow, with Justine's encouragement. She never stops him in his adventurous experiments, she simply tells him the best way to manage them.

Under a big fallen spruce, its network of dead twigs a snowy maze, Justine set two traps along the brook in the only place an animal could run by. I made a rabbit snare, working under Bruce's critical eye, and after I finished with a sigh of relief, he made me do it all over again. Justine called from ahead, "You can make a cubby here." So when I finished my snare I went to the pine where the trap and bait lay. I set up sticks, I wove balsam, I made a roof to keep off the snow. I felt quite proud of it, though perhaps it was not as compact as Justine's.

I made another snare. It was snowing hard by now, but I managed to get a perfect circle. Then Bruce informed me the loop was too big and stood by till I made it smaller. After that I made the second cubby, with Bruce telling me when I got the sticks too far apart and how to weave the balsam closer.

"You know somepin?" he said, "You haven't set the trap."

"Justine did that," I said assuredly.

"It's not set. It isn't spread open and that little thing ought to be up."

"Now, Bruce," I said patiently, "Justine knows I can't set a trap. She's taken care of it, darling." And having finished the cubby to my satisfaction, I went on, Bruce giving me up in despair and dashing ahead of me. We came home as Justine came out with buckets of dog food.

"Jus-tee-an!" Bruce shouted. "*Did* you set that last trap?"

"You did, didn't you?" I said unconcernedly.

"Hell, no," said Justine. "Didn't you?"

"Why, I don't know how to set traps!" I said. "How would I? I just built the cubbies. That's what you said to do."

"Jumpin' jimmies! you're a fine trapper! Those last three were yours."

"*Three!*" I cried.

"Sure, I just tossed the traps down by a tree, that's all I did.—Well," she said resignedly, "I'll go back after I feed Ferdinand."

"I *told* you to set them," Bruce said, accusingly.

"Everyone isn't born knowing how to set traps," I said airily. But I was quite downcast; for a brief hour I had felt so initiated.

Bill got home from his trapping line tonight and the Kerfeet spent a happy evening insulting me. Why *should* I know, I argued; I'd never even set a mousetrap.

With that, Justine took me in hand and made me set a trap, though I felt no thirst for the knowledge. The steel jaws came together with such violence they made me shiver, and with the whole family ordering me what to do with each hand and finger I didn't have time to understand why I was doing it. I was the despair of Justine; she looked at me as I'd look at a person who didn't know how to open a book and couldn't learn. "How *can* anyone be this dumb?" she wailed.

Surreptitiously I took a trap home with me and got Lee to explain it.

I practiced setting the trap. It does frighten me, for Lee is so sure I'll snap off a finger, but I cannot be disgraced in trapping circles. So finally, all alone in my little cabin, I set it. It is so ridiculously simple a baby could understand it.

When we went out on our trapping line again the first trap was sprung, and while Justine went back to get her knife I set it. Whoopla! She laughed at me for my look of profound pride.

We hitched up five dogs this afternoon. Justine wanted to take the whole six, but after Bill heard that Gus had threatened her, he said he'd rather she left him off. I felt the same way. The other five were an angelic quintet, but I think Justine was disappointed to miss the battle with Gus.

Bill helped us today by hanging on to the sled for our start, and we made the curve to the road without a spill. The dogs started off like lambs. Whittles, tied to the lead rope so he couldn't hang back, behaved beautifully, and even Wolf went with a swing. We could feel today that we had excess power.

The day was like a crisp apple, the white road was barred with brightest azure, and the dogs' furry shadows, bright blue too, sped along beside us.

The dogs ran freely, their harness bells jingling. Even uphill they went buoyantly. Once they stopped dead, but it was because they scented a deer on the hill. All five heads turned alertly at the same instant, ears up, noses twitching. They were a beautiful frieze against the snow.

The pure line of hilltop, the dark spruces cutting sharply against the flawless green sky, made me want to shout. But it was icy cold. Bruce and I walked up two long hills to warm our feet and give the dogs a rest. Whittles was lagging deplorably now, and Swede pulled him as well as the sled. But on the home stretch we had speed again.

Late last night I went out with Lee to take a long walk. In the bright moonlight we went far down the Gunflint Trail and back by the ski track. It was perfectly still. I love the deep silence of the midwinter woods. It is a stillness you can rest your whole weight against. Not the light silence of summer, constantly broken by the sound of leaves, bird-song, the scurry of little beasts, and the hum of insects. This stillness is so profound you are *sure* it will hold and last.

The trees stood without movement, and the white snow glittered with bright gold specks from the half-moon. Our narrow path led through black spruces decorated with arabesques of white. The night was only pleasantly cold.

We had seen many deer tracks but no deer. "I know," I said. "You go through the cedars along the shore, and I'll keep to the road. One of us may scare a deer toward the other." "I'd just figured that out too," Lee said, and went down through a clearing.

I kept along the white lane. The stillness was absolute. Was this really I, in a winter forest alone at midnight? It was a strange liberty to feel so disembodied in this misty glimmer. Suddenly I heard a faint crackle, very faint, and stopped short.

Out between the inky spruces leaped two deer. They took the road in one great floating bound and curved up the hill between slim aspens. They were so light, so noiseless, they might have been phantom deer. They seemed so fabulous they might have been unicorns.

December 7th

Lee is the trapper, after all. He caught a shrew in a mousetrap. This smallest quadruped is only as big as two thimbles, and certainly doesn't look like the most bloodthirsty beast in existence! Its plush fur is white underneath, its eyes are set far down its long, sensitive nose, it has cocky whiskers and the tiniest feet—insect feet.

Bill started out for his trapping shack again, carrying a huge roll of tar paper. A bear had been curious about the cabin and climbed on the roof, smashing the stove pipe and ripping off the roof covering.

Justine let me try the snowshoes she's been repairing. I've never been on snowshoes before, and of course I *would* try them on our trapping line, which is all brush and tangles, with never an inch of level space. "Just let yourself go loose and loppy," Justine said. "Don't try to lift the snowshoes; they're balanced for the tails to drag. Otherwise, walk as you always do—no longer steps. Only, when you stop, put one foot in front of the other, so you won't trip yourself when you start out again."

Bruce and I started out. I made fine progress when I concentrated on

74

my feet, but not when I thought about traps or the intelligent answers Bruce insists on having to his multitudinous questions.

At the huge fallen log one trap was sprung but the other was all right, and I decided not to disturb the set-up. As we turned away, a weasel's head darted up, then the whole little animal curved up over the snowy log. It was as white as the snow it stood on, except for the black tail tip that makes it ermine. It looked at us with its smooth, small head up-raised; its curving, wicked grace had an intense fascination. It looked so dangerous that I was very thankful it wasn't a larger animal. Suddenly, with no apparent flicker of movement, it vanished. It was as if a snow-flake melted.

Justine said to Bruce later, "How did she get along on her snow-shoes?"

"She was pretty slow," he said. "She fell down two or eight times."

It's very cold, but Patty runs out in the snow barefooted, with only her diaper and little shirt on. She also stands on the tray of her high chair, balancing like a circus rider and waving her toast debonairly in the air. She eats ashes, and corn meal from the dogs' pail, and coffee and dough, yet she has as pink cheeks and bright brown eyes as any super-sanitary baby.

December 10th

Up in the dark and over to breakfast through a snowy gale. The wind howling like a werewolf across the lake and whole drifts blowing about made the Kerfoot cottage with its orange windows glittering be-hind icicles look very inviting. "*Nobody* can make me go outdoors to-day," I told myself.

As Justine and I were having our usual after-breakfast coffee before doing the dishes, Lee came in. "Come out and see this wind!" he urged.

Dawn was coming. Scarlet argosies careened across a yellow sky over the black water. There was a great noise of wind-lashed trees. I ran home to put on heavier clothes and then pushed against the rush of air, down to the lake.

The ice floes, blown from the frozen bays, were crackling against our shores. I could hardly stand against the wind. When I took shelter behind the drifts at the lake's edge, one step would be clear, at the next I'd go in to my waist. Tears blinded me.

When I could see at all, it was worth the struggle. Magnetic Bay, which was frozen over, looked as if it were a plain filled with geysers; the snow swept straight up in whirling columns. Big triangles and blocks of ice were hurled up on our shore. Down the bay the white birches on the white hills were swept over almost to the blue-black water. Occasionally the wind gave a piercing scream.

The sun came over the hill just as I got back to our cabin, frozen, gasping, and breathless. Do you know what the husband who had been so eager for me to see the wind was doing? Sitting at ease by the warm stove, making a drawing of it!

Today Ferdinand fell off the dock, trying to get a drink. After rescuing him, though why she bothered I don't know, for he only went to eating snowshoes, Justine baked bread. She wraps it in oiled paper and puts it in the cupboard outside the door to freeze; when it is thawed it's like fresh bread. The bacon and ham are in boxes on the porch roof, and woodpeckers and chickadees are always investigating them, while I remember the hairy woodpecker's tongue.

Indoor work is so unnatural to Justine that to see her keeping house is just like having a wild deer in the kitchen. At any minute I expect her to strike out with small hoofs, leap through the window, and disappear into the woods!

Bruce was very funny at breakfast. Evidently the flood of adult conversation has begun to bore him, and he is determined to have his turn. "You know somepin?"—his favorite opening—and "Just a minute, Bill!" in the reproving tone Bill sometimes employs, "Par'n me, *I'm* talking." And, "Remind me to tell you about my beaver when I finish this story." He caught a beaver last spring when he was just four, and skinned it himself; there are movies to prove it. His eyes grow *very* round when he tells an adventure, his long lashes curl with excitement, and his cheeks get brilliant.

This kitchen is very small for six in the family, and when you add a few guests, Ferdinand with his head in the door in an attempt to get a drink from our water barrel, and the cat and puppies roving in and out, it is full to repletion.

Sometimes when this happens, and Patty, after sitting comfortably in the bucket of ashes, splatters raspberry jam on walls and chairs and throws her cereal on the floor; when Bruce's wad of clay and his cherished beaver claws get mixed in with the crackers and cheese, and some socks lie on the ham and the dogs' pail of corn meal and scraps comes perilously near to boiling over into the soup, I want to give a loud scream and rush out into the middle of a vast, open, *empty* plain.

But usually the kitchen is a gay little place, and we have such a good time at the table that we linger over every meal as if it were our last. Certainly we couldn't have been luckier in finding congenial hosts. When we considered this winter, one of the things I wondered about was how we'd find enough to talk about for such a length of time, with strangers. But we never have any difficulty here!

And I certainly have the greatest respect for what the women living on the Trail accomplish. Everything takes so long, dressing, building fires, getting wood, carrying water, baking bread. When Bill is gone, Justine also has the light plant and the animals to look after. The laundry takes forever, for all the water has to be carried in pails from the lake.

Sometimes when all this gets too overpowering, Justine gets glowery —owly, she calls it. Thunderclouds much too big for her hang Jovelike about her brow and fall down over her straight nose. She looks like Patty then, and gets over her black mood just as quickly.

December 13th

Twenty below, and a fierce north wind. This is the coldest kind of weather you can have, Justine says; subzero temperatures aren't so bad if it's calm. Still the lake is not frozen, though it's been cold enough for many days now; the wind is too strong to allow it.

It is very interesting to me to hear about these lake temperatures. It seems that all summer the main mass of lake water is motionless, only the surface water being moved by the wind and current. But as the surface gets colder in the fall, there are vertical currents, the cold surface water sinks, the lower water rises until the whole lake is cold, and then the surface freezes. Here it usually freezes around the tenth of December, and we are getting very impatient!

We now have to carry water from the dock, where a waterhole is kept open. To my surprise, the barrel stove keeps our cabin perfectly comfortable. I've grown very fond of our little stove; it does not even seem ugly any more. The knowledge that we can live happily in this one-room cabin is a fine acquisition.

Our doorknobs freeze to our hands, so I made them little shirts of red cheesecloth, to Bruce's amusement. This is his fifth birthday, by the way. He said last night, "Justine, when are you going to make the birthday?" He has never had anyone to ask to a birthday party, so he thinks the cake is the birthday.

Mr. Stapleton just called on the phone and Just was very sympathetic. "Hell, that's a shame!" she kept saying. Hanging up, she said offhandedly, "George has been chasing a wolf all yesterday and today. It got away with his trap and toggle, and today after chasing the thing around three lakes he found the trap with one toe in it, right at his lodge! He's so mad I didn't dare kid him." Just as if hunting a wolf two days in this weather were a most ordinary occupation!

December 14th

The lake has frozen at last. Now we are in deep winter.

The wind blew hard all last night, but at some time there must have been a few minutes' lull, for when we left the Kerfoots after a spirited game of Chinese checkers and eleven o'clock coffee, the lake was a white

78

expanse. It has been at freezing temperature for so long that a short respite from the wind was enough. The Kerfoots say they have never known it to freeze over all at once like this; usually one end is frozen hard while you can still use a boat at the other.

This morning we rose at eight with bright moonlight streaming in our west window, the moon high in the sky. It is twenty-nine below! Justine gave me moccasins to wear over three pairs of socks. Oh, the lovely *free* feeling, to get out of those heavy boots! It is like going barefoot, only pleasanter.

When we went over to breakfast, "Thirty below!" I cried, as we tripped over puppies and brushed Ferdinand aside to get into the warm kitchen.

"Twenty-nine," Lee corrected.

"Oh, *Lee!*" I said. "Let's talk in round numbers—thirty sounds so *much* more interesting!"

"As a matter of fact," he said, unrelenting, "the mercury has divided. It's probably not quite twenty-nine." So ever since he has called it twenty-eight below, in spite of maledictions and entreaties.

With great trepidation, I went out on our trap line. It was too cold for Bruce, which shows how really courageous I was. By the lake the wind was so keen I realized the word "deadly" was no exaggeration. It stung even inside my forehead. I felt it against my eyeballs inside the lids.

The frost is so deep on the trees, it is uncanny. Every bit of landscape—spruces, cedars, pines—is dead white, and every twig is heavy with frosted crystals. These frosted trees have an *exact* purity, whereas snow gives them a blurred, softened look. Now every detail is emphasized, every line precise.

The little entrances of burrows are now lovely things, all hung with enormous frost feathers where the warmer air of the tunnel meets the cold; entrancing doorways to a secret world. I wonder if I would *ever* get bored with the outdoors here! It never seems even commonplace. I am conscious of strange, vivid life all around me; I move through its mystery.

The rabbits seem to have had dances in the bright moonlight, flitting in the most airy manner on their big, fluffy feet; their tracks show incredible bounds across the ice-bound brook. Our lovely trap line seems to be a series of feeding stations for mink and mice. I'm certain my joy in it would be spoiled if we ever caught anything, but that is a dark secret. I am reasonably conscientious about repairs; it is only occasionally that I deliberately put the herring in a harmless spot.

When I came home, relieved at still possessing my fingers and toes Lee was working on paintings of South Sea birds, from skins sent him from the museum. Red and yellow parrots, fruit pigeons with violet and rosy feathers, brilliant honey eaters—such a tropic array, with icicles outside and the lake groaning and booming! Butchie and Bobby, who came over by dog sled to see us, were fascinated by the strange birds; Butchie handled them with adoring fingers.

The coldest morning yet. The lake was so cold it looked dead, and the sky was as empty of color as a glass of water, except for the faintest tinge of rose in the north. The puppies came in frosted like little cakes, and the cat had the most grotesque expression with heavy white eyebrows and masterful whiskers. When I put on my snowshoes and walked down the road the lake gave out great clangs like an enormous gong. Egi was up on his kennel, howling with his nose to the sky; his breath, going straight up, froze in the air.

December 16th

Up to zero—really comfortable again. Why, I can remember a time at Gunflint when I thought zero was chilly! Justine, with an axe to test the ice, went across the lake to meet George, who wanted something for his beaver trapping.

I followed her tracks later in the day. It gave me a wonderful feeling of freedom to get out on that vast level expanse in moccasins! The reason the lake is so pure a white is that the ice is covered with frost crystals almost like sphagnum moss, lovely to see and delicate to walk on. They do not crunch loudly as the snow does now; it is a more fragile sound. I felt I'd never want to stop walking on them. Near shore they were clustered like little shuttlecocks of swan feathers. Here the cedars cast lavender shadows, and across them a line of fox tracks ran.

December 17th

Charlie Olsen was bobbing for fish, so I said to Justine, "Can't we try?" On land the wind was warm and gusty, but Justine streaked off to the center of the lake, and when we got out from the shelter of the land the wind was bitter. Bruce blew like a leaf across the ice.

Justine had a long ice chisel with which she chipped through the black ice to make a hole in which Bruce bobbed his fishline up and down. I chipped a hole, scooping the icy chips from the water with my hands—the coldest thing I ever did—and Justine made herself one. The wind swept right through us; a windbreaker was a misnomer.

On some lakes they drag out little fishhouses on runners, and fish in those, using a five-pronged spear. I certainly wished we were trying that (a stove is part of the equipment) as Justine told me to crouch low, to make a ball of myself so that I would not be so vulnerable to the wind. It was too cold to stay long, and we went home fishless. Charlie had caught five large pike and presented us with one. The wind pressure has broken the ice near his place, he says; there is a crack eighteen feet wide.

Late in the afternoon we drove to Loon Lake to pick up Bill, who was helping the Stapletons with their ice (all these resorts harvest ice for summer use) in return for George's help with the wood. People are really neighbors on the Trail!

At Loon Lake steep hills slanted to the circle of white lake, and a little clump of buildings stood deep in snow. Big blocks of transparent turquoise were in long rows along the shore, the square of water from which this ice had been cut was a shimmering, greenish black, and around it people in bright costumes were scattered, the men cutting and dragging the squares of ice, the girls fishing in the open water. The colors were so fresh and clear, the crystal air showed each least detail so perfectly, the scene gave the effect of a Persian miniature.

The ice here was seventeen inches thick, and they were cutting the cakes almost square. Sometimes the men sawed ahead of them, and sometimes they put the saw between their feet and sawed backward; they were less likely to slip that way.

The cakes were put in the icehouse exactly as they were taken from the water, so they fitted without any air spaces. After the ice is in, sawdust is packed around the sides and top to insulate it. Some people use the sphagnum moss instead of sawdust.

December 19th

We awoke to the booming of the lake, a symphony performed entirely by kettledrums. Clouds were galloping through the treetops. We found fresh tracks, sharply cut, where a doe and a fawn had walked around our cabin in the night, perhaps trying to see us, just as we try to see them.

We had planned to go over to the trapping shack with Bill today,

82

but he had to go to town to see a dentist about a tooth, and didn't get home till midnight.

His car stuck eleven times in the drifts, trees blew across the Trail, and in town the car broke down and it took four hours to locate a mechanic. The tooth had to be pulled. On the way home Bill found the telephone wire down; while he repaired that, the car froze up. "Ah me," he said blithely, "you have to have one of these days every winter. Now this is behind me!"

We made an interesting discovery today. The hairy woodpecker that has been drilling so industriously at the outdoor cupboard changed his drilling place as Justine moved the meat from lower to upper shelf. Ornithologists have been undecided whether he locates grubs by sense of smell or hearing; this seems definite proof of a sense of smell.

December 21st

The shortest day of the year.

"Fifteen below," Bill said, coming in to breakfast.

"It must be dropping," said Lee. "I made it fourteen."

"Now listen!" I cried. "You stop belittling our temperatures! It's fifteen with a fierce wind, and somebody told me you can take off thirty degrees for that, so it's really forty-five below!"

"You can't record temperature *that* way," Lee said severely, "you go by the thermometer."

"Not me," I told him. "I'm scientific; I take everything into consideration!"

In whatever temperature it was, we started off with Bill to the trapping shack. Nobody seemed to think we shouldn't, so we went.

I dressed in my heaviest clothes and went to ask Justine whether I should wear moccasins or boots. She looked me over. "Now," she said, "this is not going to be any sissy-pants trip. You'll be all right if *everything* you wear is all right; otherwise not."

So she took me in hand. She gave me her extra pair of wool pants, which were lined, and insisted I wear her rubber pacs, which are smaller than my outsize ones and not so clumsily shaped, with one pair of long wool stockings and three pairs of heavy wool socks, besides felt innersoles. She said my ski jacket was no good, for it had a windbreaker lining and the wool outside did nothing to keep me warm. Besides, the jacket was tight-fitting. So we discarded that, and I wore my plaid shirt tucked in and her shirt loosely over it, as a jacket. Then my light windbreaker parka over all. Wool mittens with leather over-mittens, a stocking cap and scarf. Snowshoes, the light packsack. There I was. I could still move.

Two men who were clearing the Trail of fallen trees gave us a lift to the Rib Lake Trail. Getting out of the truck there and putting on our snowshoes, I felt a little apprehensive, for the road crew had seemed slightly surprised at our outing, but as soon as we got under way I forgot all my fears.

In the deep woods, away from the savage wind, the day was glorious. The low sun (which we see for only six hours now) cast a pale gold light on the snow, as if it were sunset instead of midday. The snow lay about us unmarred except for the myriads of animal tracks, some casual, some denoting a deadly purpose, others only queer little irrelevancies. I enjoyed venturing into this region of unseen life.

On a little lake, Bill had placed a fox trap on a big beaver house, since a fox likes to stand on an eminence to survey the landscape for his prey, and we looked at that and at a series of mink traps. Then we came to pine forest.

This was real adventure, snowshoeing into deep winter. And I was relieved that I was getting along so well on my snowshoes. I had read of agonizing cramps from them. But Bill said that was from walking too tensely. So when I grew tired I walked with an extreme loppiness, and that rested me.

Up along a cliff, Bill stopped to fasten the parka hood close about his face.

"We're coming to the lake?" Lee asked.

"That's right. It's a mile across the lake after we go down the cliff here. Sit on the tails of your snowshoes and slide!"

It sounded impossible, but it was fun, though I tangled with a small spruce at the bottom. The lake really did look menacing with the snow whirling across it. "It's not more than a mile," Bill repeated.

A mile in the face of that wind! "Here we go!" Until now, Bill had swung along easily, slow but steady; now he really struck out.

84

The wind cut us with icy whips. I wrapped my face in my scarf, but my panting soon made the scarf a veil of ice. Tears blinded me. When I took off a mitten to get a handkerchief my hand got stiff before I could get the mitten on again. Lee tried to take a picture, but the camera shutter wouldn't click and his hands almost froze. "Keep making faces," he yelled at me. "Keeps the circulation going there."

Bill stopped behind a point that jutted into the lake to look at a trap, and we staggered after him. "We made 'er!" he said. "Just another jog now."

What a psychologist! For we started out with renewed vigor. The jog was far longer than I'd expected, but we were in the lee of an island for awhile. Then a last sprint across a white channel and we reached the shelter of pines.

"Whew, that was something, huh?" Bill asked us.

But I feel as if I'd won a battle, I thought. There was a triumphant spirit about us. I'd far rather fight this wind and cold, I decided, than shop in Christmas mobs all day and go home on the subway in the rush hour!

It was deep forest on this point, and late afternoon. Only a few spots of gold sun shone down through the dark shadows. Suddenly, "There she is," said Bill. The trail curved, and in a little hollow, sheltered by pines, stood the smallest log cabin I ever saw.

"She's down in a hollow, you see, sheltered from the wind. Seven by nine, that's all she is!" The cabin had one window, a small door, and a little stovepipe sticking cockily from the low roof. Bill ushered us inside.

The three of us *could* get in, but if two wanted to move the third had to sit on the bunk. This was a double bunk of split jackpine poles, with a single bunk above it, so you could sit on the lower and use the upper as a backrest. A tiny table was nailed against the wall and the smallest stove in the world stood in one corner. The remaining space was about three feet square.

"We'll have coffee first," Bill said hospitably, "then I'll get balsam for the bunks."

"I love to gather balsam," I said. "Let me do that."

"What queer ideas people have of pleasure!" Bill marveled. "It seems to me I've spent my life rushing around after balsam in the dark. Better put on your moccasins, while I make the fire; it will rest you to get your boots off."

I took off my boots, which were coated inside with ice. My socks and feet, however, were warm and dry. "Is it balsam, not spruce?" I asked. "Wouldn't the round spruce make a thicker mat than the flat balsam?"

"Lady, spruce needles needle right through your blankets. I haven't any eiderdown sleeping bag for myself; you get me balsam."

We had sandwiches and strong hot coffee, and felt very snug. When we found that the dirt floor was white with frost and scattered drops of water stood up on it like white peppermints, we made footstools from sticks of stove wood.

Bill walked down to the lake to chop a waterhole, Lee went to chop wood, and in the snowy forest I picked balsam boughs to my heart's content. I brought a large armload in just as Bill came with the water.

"Know how much we need? Just ten times that!" he said.

"You can't make me mad. I love the smell and feel and look of balsam."

"There's an easy way to carry it, though. See this stick with a fork near the bottom? Just stack the boughs on it, one above another—the fork keeps them from slipping off. You can carry a lot that way."

The sunset glittered in bits of gold and red through the thick pine branches, and then it was dark. Our shack looked tinier than ever, rather like a good little teakettle with the smoke rising like steam from its spout.

Inside we had a delightful atmosphere of candlelight, one candle balancing on a shelf, the other on a slab stuck in the wall. We padded the bunks deep with balsam and laid boughs on the frosted floor. Ice had already formed in the water pail next to the stove.

Dinner was soon ready. Such a minute stove, and yet I made hot spaghetti (from a can, but good) with tomato sauce and cheese, bacon, buttered carrots (dehydrated), and chocolate pudding. Because of the smallness of the stove, we had to have after-dinner coffee, but that only lent an air of elegance to the occasion.

The wind was rising outside, its roar grew louder and louder. We played cards and managed to stay half awake till nine o'clock.

Going to bed wasn't difficult. We just took off our boots. I went to sleep as soon as I crawled into the sleeping bag.

I was waked by a mouse scrabbling behind my pillow, which was my jacket and had a small piece of chocolate in its pocket. I yipped loud enough so that he never came back. The wind was roaring in the trees now, great gusts of iciness shook our bit of a cabin. Such a tiny box to shelter us in such an immensity of cold!

Sleepily, I heard an animal on the roof. What *could* be that big? . . . Oh yes, it was Bill, in the bunk above.

"Stop that jumping around upstairs!" I told him. When he moved, balsam needles rained down on us through the pine poles. "Mice in my hair," he muttered.

Our bunk was quite comfortable and the sleeping bags kept us warm. But icy arrows shot through every smallest chink. I had to wear my stocking cap, and Lee put on his hunting cap; against the faint glow from the stove his profile looked very alert. The balsam boughs were wonderfully fragrant around us.

In the middle of the night Bill suddenly bounced from his bunk.

The fire had gone out. He lit the candle and Lee tried to look at his watch, which was frozen fast to the water pail and had to be pried off.

"Two o'clock, and a fine frosty morning!" we told Bill. "Nothing like a few early morning exercises, my boy."

"Oh, it can't be more than thirty below," Bill said airily. "Don't you want to get up? Don't you want a good fresh drink of water?"

The wind was fighting the trees to the death just outside. Every other minute it would scream like a banshee, and then a tree would crash down somewhere in the forest. "Thirty below," I thought proudly, "and this is the worst wind yet. That makes it at least sixty below, but don't tell Lee. I'm glad to report it's sixty below and rapidly getting belower. . . ." I went to sleep.

We woke to morning light, yellow and cold. Bill served us breakfast, if not in bed, at least on the bunk. Hot oatmeal with raisins, pancakes and bacon and coffee. Never a better breakfast.

Then Bill started off on his trapping line; he would be gone all day, and then make the seven miles home after dark. We followed his trail a short time, and found evidence that he had aroused some spruce grouse from the snow where they'd been sleeping. The round holes from which they'd flown, with their distinct wing marks on each side, looked as if a flock of cherubs had just taken off.

We started home about eleven. It was much colder than yesterday. The white channel between the woods was blurred with frost and the lake looked most formidable. Sheets of snow eddied into the pale air and ran along like active daytime ghosts. Our snowshoe tracks of yesterday stood high above the surface, and shadows were a queer bright purple.

The wind at our backs pushed us along, but its bite cut through our heavy clothes and swept the frost along, knee-high, until we felt we were wading in an intangible river. After we crossed the lake it was difficult to get up the cliff on our snowshoes, but, pulling ourselves up by bushes, we made the top and took a deep, satisfied breath. The worst was over.

The walk home seemed far longer than yesterday's, but we enjoyed it. The only time we grew really cold was when I decided we should stop for hot tea! We nearly froze getting that hot tea. Our sandwiches were stiff with ice. My mittens were frozen, and while Lee tried to thaw them out my hands and feet got so numb I was really frightened.

When we started out again I tore along the trail till I began, little by little, to grow warm again. Only my feet took a long time to come to life.

But in spite of the intense cold—no, because of it, for it was an adventurous feeling to pit oneself against it—we reveled in this world, freshly modeled by last night's wind. All its contours were changed, fluffed and recurved and shining new. Even the shadows were full of life. From a spruce thicket we heard the sweet, clear notes of the pine grosbeak. This melody would be welcome at any time, but now, when the few noises heard are harsh or hollow, its loveliness is incredible, especially as the massive silence of winter intensifies every sound.

Nothing else would have stopped me in my mad career, but we had to see that bird. We finally found him, the beauty, in a snowy spruce top. His feathers were as vivid a rosy red as if he were carved from pure flame; his gray mate with a yellowish cap seemed much more a denizen of earth.

When we reached home Butchie had come back from her trapping, and she gave us a beaver dinner. The strong meat has to be parboiled in two waters and cooked with sage and onions to moderate the strong flavor. This was the grown beaver, and the taste comes from the poplar bark it consumes; the young ones are tender, and the beaver tail and liver are accounted great delicacies. The meat we had was good, but not delicious as venison is. Venison we can eat day after day and not tire of it.

Bill came in late tonight, rather disgruntled because he'd had a chance at a wolf and missed it. While he was kneeling on the ice getting a mink from a trap, he had a feeling that eyes were upon him. He turned slowly and there was a wolf standing over on the shore, staring at him. Evidently he didn't recognize a man in the doubled-up position and was wondering what animal it was. Bill was so surprised that he made the mistake of grabbing his gun, instead of reaching for it gradually, and the wolf made off.

December 23d

We decided to get ready for Christmas today; the Chippewa families are coming over for dinner. We brought the turkey in to thaw, and made cakes, and Bruce and I strung cranberries and popcorn for the tree. I haven't done that since I was very small.

At sunset Bruce and Lee and I started up the cliff trail to get a Christmas tree. It was a delight to have such thousands to select from, but almost impossible to choose among them. On a ridge we found a beauty, and I begged a tiny one besides. I've always wanted to have a Christmas tree for birds. Coming down, the spicy air and the great snowy landscape were so inspiriting that Lee and I surprised Bruce by bursting into carols. The lake was a giant mosaic in pastel colors as the sunset reflected on various surfaces. It was as if a rainbow had been shattered there.

Since everyone will be in for their Christmas mail tomorrow, we decorated the tree tonight. All of us, that is, except Justine, who chose this evening to skin Bill's mink and weasel. She varies, from almost the "ugly little wench" Bill affectionately calls her, to vivid attractiveness; tonight she looked demure and charming, sitting by the birch fire with her horrid little raw carcasses, which confronted me whenever I looked away from Christmas tinsel and lights. Patty ran around in a big straw hat and very little else, and Bruce was determined never to go to bed. "Don't look at me, by any chance," he told Bill.

December 24th

A delicious day, crisp but not cold, and I always love the day before Christmas better than Christmas itself. I put our birds' Christmas tree outside the west windows on a tall stump and decorated it with jackpine cones dipped in melted suet, strings of popcorn and cranberries, small bright apples, and birch-bark cornucopias filled with fat and sunflower seeds. A scarlet Christmas ornament shone on the tip. It looked very festive.

Everyone for miles around came for the mail. Ahbutch came across the ice with her dogs, pulling a rowboat she had borrowed in the summer. We decorated Ferdinand with a mammoth bow of scarlet oilcloth and dog-sled bells, which he wore with a quiet perplexity.

When the Wilderness Express arrived it was spilling over with Indian boys, packages, and mail. A gorgeous toboggan was tied on top of the truck, skis and snowshoes were mixed with groceries. We had an orgy with letters and Christmas cards, but Justine confiscated all our packages. Don drove on to Saganaga, though everyone told him it was impossible to get through; the family there had to have their Christmas presents.

After everyone left we ate a hasty supper, arranged the packages around the tree, and had Christmas eggnogs, while carols from radio archangels rang around us. It was a lovely Christmas Eve.

As we went home through the night, we saw Ferdinand curled in his little shed, with one puppy between his knees and another on his back, while the red bow still gleamed beneath his chin.

Around our cabin, the aspens seemed to stretch heaven high. They had an unearthly dimension, like trees of legend in whose boughs hung

little golden worlds. I remembered that in *The Heart of Nature*, Sir Francis Younghusband suggests that there may be higher beings than ourselves on these sparkling stars, and "among those higher beings higher qualities than any we know of, or can conceive, may have emerged." What fun to imagine, as I look at this still beauty about us, that the joy, the tenderness, and good will that we human beings feel most of all on this Eve, are only crude intimations of what may be experienced!

Christmas Day

It is thirty *above!* Scandalous! This isn't the Christmas weather we are supposed to endure!

After breakfast Bruce distributed the presents, glittering like the Christmas tree in his excitement. Later, the Indians arrived by dog team and Charlie Olsen came along. My family had sent Christmas crackers in our box of gifts, and everyone wore the gay paper caps. The Indians love any sort of fun and frolic. I wish I had a picture of old Charlie and Butchie's mother in their carnival hats.

Nettahwense is a wonderful old woman, with much character in her face. She is shy, but she has great poise. Justine says nobody else can make one feel as awkward as an Indian can. She told me, as we were getting dinner, of going over to ask Nettahwense what moss to use to chink this cabin.

Of course neither one could talk to the other, but they made signs. Justine, however, could not understand, and finally Nettahwense was through. Then, try as Justine would to get her attention, she remained oblivious. To Nettahwense Justine simply wasn't there. Justine finally had to give up in despair and slink off home.

I liked listening to the Indians talking together. Chippewa holds the same place in Indian languages as French has held in European; it is the language of courtesy and grace.

While we ate the turkey dinner, Charlie Olsen told us about his boyhood in Norway, herding cattle above the timberline. Patty, busy with the boxes of chocolates, paid no attention to the dinner or the toys. In the middle of the festivity Ferdinand stuck his head in the door, like a goblin spirit of Christmas.

94

We have been lucky in escaping the flu which has swept the North Shore, but now Justine and I have both caught colds. The Indians on this lake are very considerate; since they have learned from the Kerfoots that colds are contagious, they don't come in when they have them and stay away when the Kerfoots do. However, one of the Chippewa boys who came up on the Wilderness Express the day before Christmas was a stranger, and unfortunately it was he who had a cold. He also had a banjo and entertained us in the kitchen; I wish he'd serenaded us from outside!

I've spent most of the day in bed, watching the birds at their Christmas tree. The whiskeyjacks and one blue jay came first, and gobbled like mad. They have an exasperating charm! Then the hairy woodpeckers, in white plush and gleaming black. They are supposed to be solitary through the winter, but here the male and female came together. A timid downy came hesitantly now and then. Last of all, the chickadees flew in daintily. One Hudsonian chickadee, with a reddish glint to his feathers and a brown cap instead of a black one, sat in a little bower of cranberry and popcorn garlands.

The hairy woodpeckers had a terrific struggle with the dangling suet, for there was nothing for them to hammer against. Finally the male flew beneath and grabbed it in his claws, clasping it to his breast, while his tail stuck straight up at right angles. Holding it in a vise like that, he proceeded, upside down, to drill into it.

I went to the cottage for dinner, to find Bruce in bed in disgrace. He had built a small bonfire and thrown a puppy into it. "There are savage depths in all men"; my Bruce is no exception. Though I really think, aside from the day-after-Christmas mood, that it was a scientific experiment. Result, one puppy slightly singed and one small boy in bed. *Quite* unjustly, the small boy thinks; he is in a black sulk, and Patty runs in to pat him comfortingly.

It's snowing. Justine and I made snowflake molds all afternoon. I'd read last winter in *Natural History* that it was possible, but I could never get the chemical—the polyvinyl formal resin in ethylene dichloride. (You'd think *that* would be easy to find!) Now a museum friend has sent a small bottle, and we've caught snowflakes all afternoon.

I've felt far more thrilled than if we were catching mink or ermine. It is marvelous to gaze as long as we like at the intricate hexagonals, instead of having them vanish in an instant. We kept running with especially magnificent trophies to Bill and Lee, who looked with mild interest but none of our ecstasy. "O filigree petal," Francis Thompson says,

> *So purely, so palely,*
> *Tinily, surely,*
> *Mightily, frailly,*
> *Insculped and embossed,*
> *With His hammer of wind,*
> *And His graver of frost.*

I can never forget the utter clarity of these winter dawns. The complete *stainlessness* in the coloring of early morning is what affects me most deeply. What did I say, when the snow first fell, about the monotony of white landscapes?

These subtle colors have no richness, but a strange and deliberate power. The infinite gradations of faint rose, clear blue, or pale gold over the vast stretches of snow come from no frailty, but from a hidden strength such as a pearl has. The purity of line, too—however fragile it may be, it is distinct and sure. These simplicities of curve and shadow make me feel that they are preliminary sketches of a fresh earth made just before I came upon them.

This morning the ice was a frail amber color, changing to soft grass-green in the shadow of the hills. The sky was made of transparent and delicate beryl, and the hills were dusky dark.

"Let's go on an all-day trip with the dogs!"

Justine agreed to take us, and after breakfast we put up a lunch and harnessed the dogs.

Egi went wild. His four feet were never on the ground, and his wild wail echoed far along the Gunflint shores. Swede, harnessed first, barked steadily from that moment until we started out.

The dogs had not been driven since before Christmas, and they were rampant with joy. We started downhill with Bill at the head of the team, Lee holding Egi (the most distracted), and Justine pulling back on the sled handles. I was on the sled, slightly aghast.

The dogs *leaped* down the hill—Lee could hardly keep his feet against Egi's surges—and we bumped and jerked over the broken ice, onto the lake. There Bill left us, and we started out gaily. But Justine didn't like the harness arrangement and stopped the team. Immediately Loppy and Whittles sprang at each other.

Justine grabbed the lead dog, Lee seized the sled handles, stretching out the team to keep the other dogs from joining the fight, while I scrambled off the sled.

"Kick them apart," Justine shouted. I hesitated. "Here, take Swede." Justine had no club, but she yanked the dogs apart. Loppy flew in again and clamped his teeth at the root of Whittles's tail. Whittles gave a scream of agony.

Justine kicked and pulled at Loppy. To no avail; his jaws were like steel. Whittles, stretched on the ice, was writhing. Justine, getting a hold on Loppy's windpipe, though that was almost impossible through his heavy hair, had to choke him nearly to death before he at last let go.

Whittles lay as if dead, on his back with his paws limply curled. All his glorious beauty was gone. Justine got him up on his feet somehow. "He's not seriously hurt, thank goodness. It's mostly his pride—he couldn't get his teeth in Loppy." His hindquarters were red with blood, blood ran down his neck from a torn ear. I thought we'd take him home. But no, on we went.

Soon the dogs swung into their stride and ran along intoxicated with the shining morning. The little harness bells jingled gaily, and the furry shadows of the dogs, bright blue on the snow, seemed to jingle too. The lake stretched wide before us, broken by a big pressure ridge, where the ice, forced up by its expansion, had cracked and frozen again. It was like a great frozen breaker, five feet high in places, but we found a safe spot to cross and sped on.

We came at last to pine knolls with a bay back between them. We tied the dogs in a cedar swamp and climbed a high dome, up through deep drifts between spruces. Here we had a magnificent view up and down the blue ice and white snow.

Across the snow we saw wolf tracks, many of them, and also the track of another dog team; some Indians had come back from Port Arthur. On the cliff itself were fox tracks. This cliff is one of the vantage points from which the foxes watch our odd activities.

Down in the bay, we took the dogs around a peninsula. Here was a comfortable place for luncheon, under thick balsams. We broke boughs for seats and built our campfire. I had forgotten the cups, so Justine made birch-bark ones as the Indians make baskets—folded like a box, with sticks split like clothespins to hold the corners tight. We melted snow for tea and toasted sandwiches.

Since Lee wanted to make some sketches of the rocks here, he said he would walk home after they were done. Justine and I started back with the dogs.

We faced the wind now. I grew cold and trotted with the dogs. The clear ice was as slippery as a fish, and the dogs skidded and spread-eagled. Whittles tired, and Swede wore himself out dragging him along.

Justine let Swede run free, putting Egi in as lead. Egi was conscientious, but he had no particular pride in his promotion. Whittles was wheel dog now, and when he lost his footing and got tangled in the harness he collapsed and let the other dogs slide him along, on his feet or on his side, he simply didn't care.

Though Justine scolded and switched him, it had no effect. Then I interfered, which one should never do; I sympathized. "Poor Whittles," I said, "You *are* having a tough day, old boy." At the affection in my voice, he practically burst into tears and tried to climb up on the sled with me. He didn't want to be big and strong and tough; he wanted with all his heart to be a lap dog.

December 31st

A gray and misty morning, rather nice after all our clear days.

Bruce and I went on our trap line. We found our first victim, a dead rabbit in a snare, frozen too stiff to look pitiful. Bruce seized him in triumph and ran off home. "You take a short cut and I'll take a long cut," he said. "I'll meet you at the wolf snare." Having caught a rabbit, he was sure we'd catch a wolf.

We went to the beaver pond too, where Bill had set a mink trap. The pond was a small circle of flawless white, ringed by steep hills. The black pines and spruces were veiled in frost and the birches and aspens were blooming with ethereal, gauzy flowers, of such fragility that apple or cherry trees would seem blatant and gaudy in comparison. The cliff behind them was white instead of black, shining like old silver, so beautiful I kept catching my breath. A steep, slanting line from the tattered spruces near us up to the high cliff was more ravishing than any curve, and the shore, where the level whiteness broke up into frosty tangles of slim branches, was like silence broken by faint music. There was no color anywhere, no hint of color. It was all a silvery monotone.

Bruce couldn't get me to pay any attention to the traps; he was quite impatient at my daydreaming.

New Year's Day

Last night was New Year's Eve, and so after the children were asleep we took to drink and gambling. We played all the games the family sent for Christmas (to aid us in our solitary confinement)—parchesi, lotto, anagrams, checkers—we played them all at a nickel a game, reveling in Cuba libres and Christmas cookies, and listening to night-club music from New York and Chicago and Port Arthur.

Suddenly, at a quarter of twelve, Justine and I thought of driving in the car across the lake to serenade the trapper and his wife. "Certainly," said our husbands, "if the car will start." They thought they were perfectly safe, but we had a minor miracle—the car started like a lamb, and at midnight we were out on the international boundary, making an attack on Canada, firing pistols, jingling dog-sled bells, clashing tin cups for cymbals, with a hundred feet of water and sixteen inches of ice under our wheels.

The Ambroses had just turned in, but they turned out again, and we sat by their blazing fire and had café royale. It was a delightful new year.

And this morning, Bruce, the cunning scamp, brought us all coffee in bed. He got up, built the kitchen fire, and brought coffee to Justine and Bill. We were still asleep when we heard the call, "Knock, knock," with which he usually announces himself, and when Lee got up to see why he was about, he came staggering in, put his huge tray on the chair by my bed, and poured my coffee for me.

January 6th

Lee and I took a morning walk across the lake. We always like to head toward Canada; it has a strong allurement for us. It is so rich and fortunate in the wilderness the United States has for the most part lost that it is an inspiring feeling just to face toward it. As Lee says buoyantly, "only three railroads and one motor road between us and the Arctic Circle!"

On the lake the ice was so beguiling that we made slow progress across it. Most of the skim of snow had blown away. Almost always the lakes are snow-covered, and in any case the surface is roughened and opaque. But this year it is clear black glass.

Today there were deep fissures all through it, sharp severances of white crystal splintered through the black—slanting, jagged, with triangles or stars. No crack stopped short at any other, apparently because the ice has an ability to weld itself completely after a break.

We found cracks that seemed to have been twisted, ropes of crystal with gauzy leaves swung out, networks of silver, garlands with crystal pendants. How I should like to know how these effects are achieved. It is unbelievable to find them in this black, solidified water! There were showers of tiny raindrops held suspended in the ice, and curved, milk-white shells. It looked perilous to walk on, all this capricious fancy, yet it was solid strength.

Sometimes in the spring thaw the ice, instead of becoming thinner, separates into long rods, with spaces between them. It is as thick as ever, but no longer a solid mass; it is honeycombed. Sometimes the rods are joined only by a thin skim of surface ice, which naturally is far too fragile to hold any weight. If you get on such a place you lie flat and try to squirm along.

We have heard many stories of cars breaking through the ice in spring. One couple, with their brother, stopped a truck in front of their cabin, and the ice broke. The brother jumped to safety, but the couple were caught in the cab. The brother telephoned a neighbor that his companions had drowned; then he changed to warm, dry clothes. When help came, they found the husband in the freezing water clinging to the ice and holding his wife, who was unconscious by that time. They had escaped from the cab, but they couldn't climb up on the ice unaided. I don't know whether to laugh or cry at the brother's subsequent predicament.

Lee has cut a huge block from a fallen white pine, up on the ski trail, to use in carving his deer head. Egi goes with him to haul; Egi is our favorite of all the sled dogs. Tonight Lee asked Bill why Egi always looks back as he goes downhill. To be sure Lee is coming? "No," said Bill, "to see if the sled will hit his legs. Pete, the smartest wheel dog we ever had, knew a good trick. When the sled threatened him, he would get his hind feet up on the bumper and run like hell on his front legs!"

January 10th

Lee has just found that he must be in New York the first of February. I thought when we came that I should be ready to leave after the holidays, but now I want the whole winter. I remembered today that I'd planned to go into Duluth off and on during our stay! I've never even thought of it since we've been here.

When Bruce and I went to the fishing holes today the wind was as ferocious as ever. I hacked away with the ice chisel, and Bruce hacked, and we both grew very irritable. We really had words. "You're a slow poke," said Bruce, "I'm a *fast* poke!" His standards are derived from Justine, who is as strong as a small pile driver, and he looked with pro-

found contempt at my industrious chipping. Finally I lay down on the ice to recover, and he left me flat. I realized suddenly that I didn't *have* to fish. I went to see Bill who had just started to cut ice.

The harvesting of ice all over this north country is a new thing to me. Bill says they have never had such beautifully clear ice, without snow or slush. He had just cut a square to see how thick it was—fifteen inches here—and laid down his saw to explain his procedure. There was a swish, and no saw. "She's gone," he said, and went on explaining his methods. I love Bill's imperturbability.

We strolled over and looked down the hole. Black water. Ice walls in a gold square. No saw. He had another, however, and soon great blocks of transparent aquamarine were standing on the shore. We all helped in the harvest, Bruce working me so hard that I was wet with perspiration. "Now you're loggin'!" he encouraged me, imitating Justine with the dogs!

Late in the afternoon I put on my snowshoes and walked down the road. A chickadee lured me down through snowy windfalls, where I tripped and fell flat in a drift. I didn't pick myself up; I lay in the snow and looked dreamily up through the green pine needles to the gray clouds racing by. I was once sure I could never enjoy winter because I could not lie still and look up into the sky!

Small aspens stood near. Gentle and tremulous as these trees look, they are intrepid explorers, ranging to the very edge of the treeless zone. I put out a hand to a slim trunk, and it felt as responsive to my fingers as the hand of a friend. I feel the life in trees now as I do the zest in animals and birds; it does not seem lessened by winter. I am sure that now I could never feel lonely in a forest.

I might have stayed horizontal for a long time if the chickadee had not been so concerned; I *had* to get up to relieve his mind.

I went home by the lake, which cracked and groaned under me till it seemed there must be a savage tribe beneath the ice, whooping and struggling and beating on war drums. The noises are astounding, especially a loud *Uhh!* which sounds as if someone just under the ice is using all his strength to break through. I must ask Butchie if the Indians have any legends about these noises.

Then I found I was pursued by snowsnakes, wriggling along the

104

white lake. Marjorie Edgar, who has done much research on this species, reports that it is certain death to meet the large ones face to face; you freeze solid as they wind themselves around you. But these smaller ones didn't even snap at my toes. However, they must have been "taking in snow through their mouths and blowing it out through a hole in their heads," for they looked remarkably misty. There were no pale blue ones, and of course, since we are near Canada, these *may* have been the snow wassets, which come out after snowstorms and attack only loggers.

When I came home I asked Bruce if he thought we could trap them or snare a bog hop, which is a mixture of beaver and moose. The head, only as large as a beaver's, but with horns like those of a moose, would be a priceless trophy for our small apartment. But Bruce did not respond. He does not approve of such talk, any more than he does of my nonsense verses.

January 18th

Lee made me wake up early and stagger, more than half asleep, outdoors to see the moon with a star just beside it, like a Madonna and Child. It was a most exquisite portrayal, she gentle and slightly worn, the baby new and sparkling.

As Bill found he could get through to Saganaga and had to see a neighbor there, we took the drive with him, and after the errand he took us on a tour of the lake.

Ice ridges broke the white levels of the lake, and the beautiful gray-violet distances were blurred by blowing snow particles. The pines were darkly shadowed. Far to the east Bill saw two deer, a doe and fawn, standing on the ice. As we came closer, they began to run, occasionally taking great floating leaps over the ice. Just for the fun of romping, it seemed. We almost headed them off, but they escaped and crossed to the next island, the fawn bounding up the icy rocks and over windfalls in gay, thistledown leaps.

Bill was jubilant. "We so seldom see deer on the lakes like this in midwinter," he said. "I'd been hoping we might find one!" Then around a point we discovered another pair.

We drove parallel to them until they reached the shore and ran into the pines. One winter the Kerfoots drove parallel to a wolf on Gunflint Lake, and Justine kept pace with his swift run, which seemed to be in slow motion since wolf and car were going at equal speed until in her preoccupation she ran into a snowbank and almost overturned. Both Justine and Bill like to make experiments with more audacity than is common, and it is interesting to find that on many of their winter trips Ahbutch has been the conservative element, the brake that has stopped them on the edge of danger.

Between two points we saw seven ravens walking sedately on the ice and, driving up, we came upon a dead deer. The men got out and found the tracks of one huge wolf and several smaller ones. They had run along the shore; the big one had gone out and hamstrung the deer, and the others had closed in.

A little later five deer crossed before us from one island to another. A big buck waited on the silvery ice, with his head lifted high, while the other deer made off into the shadow of the trees. He was a splendid sight, even though he had dropped his horns. When the others were in the woods he leaped magnificently up the shore.

We drove on between islands. The lakes are used as winter roads, for travel by snowshoes or dog teams, but it is only rarely that they are clear of drifts so that cars can be driven freely all over them. Then, for a brief time, there is a vast and liberating extension of the very few roads in this country, and car tracks are found in surprising places.

We came to car tracks that led through a narrow channel. "We've never been able to drive through here before," Bill said. "It's certainly surprising how you can go everywhere this year!"

We were looking at the vistas opening out ahead of us when Bill suddenly swerved the car to the left and shot up on the shore, to stop abruptly.

Black holes of water glittered through the white ice, just where we had been about to drive, The tracks we had been following continued on beyond the splintered places. The current had eaten away the ice since the last car had passed by. We never had a narrower escape.

But it had happened so quickly there was no time to be frightened. "It just proves you can *never* trust ice," Bill said.

The men got out and dragged dead spruce across our tracks, in case another car came along. "Well," said Bill, "we'll go home, but first I'll show you the grave of a little Indian boy who fell from a cliff. They buried him on that island."

We drove to the pine-pillared island with a crescent sand beach. Landing, we walked up a peaceful trail between pines to a level space on the hill. There was the little grave, surrounded by tall Norways. It was carefully covered with boards, and at its head a small cupboard had on its open shelves the child's playthings. His treasures—a knife, a cup, dice, a broken comb, an aspirin box, a little china dog. And in front of the grave was a small circle of stones for his campfire.

Today we finished harvesting the ice, dragging it to shore and up an improvised slide to the icehouse. That is a chunky little building, and with its high window, where Bruce was perched outside on the sawdust pile, the spruce branches drooping beyond him, it made a charming picture. Justine worked inside the house, swinging the big blocks in as if she were Hercules himself.

At four we all went up to the cottage for coffee. It was a clear, gay afternoon, and suddenly we decided to have a farewell party for the Jaques, taking our supper up the ski trail.

When the men went back to the ice, Justine and I got the supper together and went out to start the campfire. Down the road we met a car, and at the sight of Justine's red hunting cap, my red hood, and Pat's red bonnet bobbing in the tikinagan on my back, the driver drove straight into the ditch!

The car held a bride and groom who had thought the end of this trail was the deepest wilderness, and here they found us starting on a picnic to get away from domesticity! After they escaped from the ditch, to a chorus of howling dogs, they took us to the hilltop from which we took the ski trail.

We found tracks where Lee and Egi had turned off into dense forest. Here we discovered an immense uprooted pine, with a chunk chopped from its trunk, and a huge pile of fresh chips.

We built a fire, and when Bill and Lee appeared, we melted snow for coffee and started the venison stew. I went after balsam, and as I came toward the fire through the dark I was really impressed. The scene might have been three hundred years ago.

The fallen pine with snowdrifts deep about it lay in a tangle of black spruce. Flames leaped high into the night, and faces were ruddy in the bright firelight. Patty in her tikinagan screamed with hunger under a misty moon.

But after supper she suddenly became a tikinagan angel. She lay back and looked at the flames and cooed like any dove. We built up the fire and sat around it talking lazily. What you say doesn't matter around a campfire in the dark; it is the fact of companionship which is precious, as the small bright circle of firelight challenges the whole black night.

108

After we came home Lee had some letters to answer, and I went out into the moonlight again. I walked along the shore and sat in a niche of rocks for a long time. It was clear and mild and still. The hills were pure white, with canopies of black foliage, and I could see blurry, furry shadows that were snowshoe rabbits skim across the barred slopes.

The ice boomed and muttered under my feet; above the trees was a sky of greenish blue, a frail and transparent peacock color. Up on the ledge above me small things were awake and about, for there were little squeaks and cries. Mice, perhaps, or shrews. Far above us all the wind blew in the pines.

How my joy in the earth has been heightened by this winter! It is a great prize—a whole quarter of a year gained. Spring and summer and autumn I have never failed to revel in, but winter I endured; now I embrace that season too. And it is a joy with a different character and power, which awakens new responses in me.

I had grown so shaken with horror at the maelstrom of cruelty and anguish spread throughout the world that I had felt I could never find a secure footing again. Through these forest days the transition that has taken place, from tense despair to a peace that is not passive, but an active release of spirit, seems a wonder and a miracle to me. All the more because it has not come from conscious thought, but from another level, a deeper and more mysterious power.

I felt such happiness. This great country in its midnight silver, and I a part of it. I was out with the deer and the foxes and wolves, which we never see, but whose trails will be past our shore in the morning. Up the hill the partridges were asleep, and in little dens woodchucks curled snugly for the winter; great powerful fish swam under the ice beneath me.

"Home is where the heart is." Then this is home—all these hundreds of miles of solitude and silver.

January 21st

Our last day in the north woods! I long to stay till spring; perhaps some day we shall see its coming.

There are too many people to whom we hate to say good-by; Lee and I have escaped for a last walk. The country fascinates us as keenly as it did the first day of our arrival.

It is snowing today. The scent of snow is manifest. The spruce are powdered deep, the soft plumes of the great white pines are overlaid with films of silver. White flakes tumble thick and fast, brushing against my face like evanescent butterflies.

All the peace that this country has given us comes showering down around us in this heavy snowfall. Our departure, in this mood, is beautiful to me. Without a pang I see the myriad footprints, which we have made along our shore and in the ice-held forest, vanish beneath the drifting snowflakes.

Florence Page Jaques (1890–1972) and **Francis Lee Jaques** (1887–1969), one of America's greatest nature artists, wrote and illustrated eight books together. They met in New York City and were married in 1927; their honeymoon, a canoe trip through the Minnesota-Ontario Boundary Waters, was described in *Canoe Country*, published in 1938. They returned to experience "the same land in another guise" during the winter of 1943–44, and *Snowshoe Country* was published as a result in 1944. This book received the prestigious John Burroughs Medal as the outstanding nature book of the year.

Their other books are *The Geese Fly High* (Minnesota, 1939), *Birds across the Sky* (1942), *Canadian Spring* (1947), *As Far as the Yukon* (1951), and *There Once Was a Puffin and Other Nonsense Verses* (1957). Lee's autobiography, *Francis Lee Jaques: Artist of the Wilderness World,* was completed by Florence after his death and published in 1973.

Justine Kerfoot was born in 1906 in Barrington, Illinois. She moved to Gunflint Lake in 1928 and was owner and operator of Gunflint Lodge for fifty-one years until she retired in 1979. Kerfoot's life in the Boundary Waters region has fascinated readers for years, from Florence Page Jaques's accounts in *Canoe Country* and *Snowshoe Country* to Kerfoot's own book, *Woman of the Boundary Waters,* published in paperback by the University of Minnesota Press in 1994.